More Active Assemblies for Every Week

Jenny Mosley and Ross Grogan

36 assemblies for each week of the school year, grouped into themes for teaching the Social and Emotional Aspects of Learning

Positive Press

Positive Press

Published in 2006 by:
Positive Press Ltd
28A Gloucester Road
Trowbridge
Wiltshire BA14 0AA

Telephone: 01225 719204
Fax: 01225 712187
E-mail: positivepress@jennymosley.co.uk
Website: www.circle-time.co.uk

Text © Jenny Mosley and Ross Grogan
Printed 2008
ISBN **978 190 4866 343**

Photography by Viewpoint, Somerset

Printed by:
Heron Press
19-24 White Hays North
West Wilts Trading Estate
Westbury
Wiltshire BA13 4JT

Contents

How to use this book — 3

NEW BEGINNINGS — 9

The Things We Need — 10
Refreshing children's enthusiasm for learning with each other

The Meet and Greet Class — 12
Making people feel welcome

I'm a Character – Get Me Out of Here! — 14
Learning to accept a challenge

Stone Soup — 17
Great things can be achieved through collaboration

A Feeling of Calm — 20
Learning some stress-busting techniques

GETTING ON AND FALLING OUT — 23

Kaizen — 24
Using a Japanese model to find out how to solve problems

The Bee Team — 26
The life cycle of bees illustrates the value of teamwork

The Meaning of Friendship — 29
Building friendly actions into a wall of friendship

By the Light of the Moon — 31
Learning the value of sharing

Blossom the Cat — 34
Learning how to overcome feelings of anger

The Way Things Work — 37
Exploring ways to repair broken friendships

BULLYING — 41

Would You Rather...? — 43
Exploring how boost-ups and put-downs make us feel

GOING FOR GOALS — 47

Trouble with Tumble — 48
Discovering the meaning of personal responsibility

Sand — 50
Geological time provides a lesson in patience

If At First You Don't Succeed — 52
A famous author is a role model of persistence

Grass Just Keeps Growing — 54
Learning the value of resilience

Whiz-quiz — 56
Looking at how role models achieve their goals

Putting It All Together — 58
Hard work and effort get results

GOOD TO BE ME — 61

Saving Mrs Dickson — 62
A kind thought leads to a great invention

Good To Be Us — 64
Finding out how it is 'good to be me'

The Three Whys — 66
Answering questions helps us to deal with problems

The Worry Wheel — 68
Learning the value of being a good listener

Treasure Hunt — 70
Overcoming worries by staying calm

The Van That Didn't Count to Ten — 72
Learning how to control feelings of anger

CONTENTS

RELATIONSHIPS   77

The Sky House   78
Learning how to cope with life's injustices

The Smelly Sock Game   80
Learning the importance of treating everyone fairly

Let the Sunshine In   82
Showing others that you appreciate them

A Jumble of Lies   84
Demonstrating the value of honesty

The Squashed Cake   87
Learning the value of owning up and saying sorry

Tail Soup   89
Developing feelings of empathy and understanding

CHANGES   94

Only Tea-sing   95
Learning to cope with unexpected change

Training Matters   97
Exploring how to become more effective learners

Independence Day   99
Focus on becoming independent learners

Felt Pens   101
A flexible approach can help to solve problems

Midsummer's Day   104
Appreciating the power of a positive attitude

Who Likes Apples?   106
Learning to cope with unwelcome change

Why SEAL Assemblies?

Assembly time is a wonderful opportunity to strengthen a cohesive whole-school approach to social and emotional aspects of learning (SEAL). Pro-social behaviour originates in the moral values that any society upholds but, in Britain, we live in a multi-cultural, multi-faith place. SEAL is a useful way of communicating the values that all of the major religions share – kindness, honesty, gentleness and so on. The 36 assemblies are designed to fit the table of themes in each SEAL pack. Don't be afraid to change any of the formats to suit your particular environment. The 'Reflection' phase can easily be changed into a prayer, for instance.

Children's level of maturity and their ability to understand social and emotional skills is very wide, so we have written the assemblies in a range of styles, some suited to younger children and some to older ones. All of them provide easily accessible ideas but you will be able to build on them in any way that you feel is appropriate for your age group and context.

The Education Act (1944) requires that Collective Worship should be 'wholly or mainly of a broadly Christian character' but that their precise nature will depend on 'the family background, ages and abilities of pupils'. The assemblies in this book are written to teach social and
emotional competencies and are not, as they stand, acts of collective worship. We have written assemblies that reflect the moral values and teaching of all the major faiths without mentioning any of them directly.

This strategy gives all of you, whatever the dominant faith in your school, a way of strengthening children's understanding of living in a caring community, together with the option to alter any of the assemblies to suit your particular needs. Don't be afraid to make changes or incorporate references to stories from religious texts. The assemblies here are for you to use in whatever way you choose.

Are you ready?

You are the key to unlocking children's hearts during assembly time. Taking an assembly demands a level of energy and vibrancy. You can get yourself into the right frame of mind, before you walk on stage, by using the following strategy, which we call 'Bin it, Bag it, Bring it'.

Bin it... There may be something that affects you personally which you need to put in the imaginary bin because there is nothing you can do about it. For example, maybe you were tailgated on the way to school, you opened up a nasty bill, or a member of staff is off sick. The only way to get through the day is to let it go completely.

Bag it... There are some issues which you need to zip up into an imaginary bag so that you can deal with it later, e.g. a row with your adolescent daughter before school, a worry about one of the pupils, a timetabling problem. You know it needs to be dealt with – but it must be zipped up until a specific time when you can take it out and totally focus on it.

Bring it... What are you bringing in to the hall that is going to lift anybody? Did you get a good night's sleep, so that you are refreshed? Did you get up a little earlier to create a golden moment for yourself in a peaceful kitchen or a garden? Did you listen to some beautiful music on the way in? What experience did you create for yourself that enables you to inspire and energise others? You cannot keep giving out to people unless you put back into your own personal reserves.

Try to get to the hall early and check that everything is ready before the children arrive. Here is a checklist to help you ensure that nothing will go wrong:

- Have you read the script thoroughly?
- Have you made notes of any alterations you have decided to make?
- Can you reach all your equipment easily?
- Have you found some appropriate music?
- Have you chosen a suitable song? Is the tape/pianist ready?
- Do you need performance space? Is there room for volunteers to come forward and do whatever you want them to do?
- Will the audience be able to see everything that is happening without straining their necks and pushing other children out of the way?
- Is your visual focus big enough to be seen/read by the children at the back? Will they be able to hear you?
- Have you allowed yourself a few moments to calm yourself before everyone arrives?

Are you focused?

Each individual needs to feel that there is space in your school for them to exercise self-expression, listen and receive acknowledgment for their efforts. Assembly is an opportunity for staff to help children feel that their school has a strong identity and they are an important part of the group. This is especially valuable for children who have only a limited experience of structure and routine in their lives away from school.

Before you start your assembly, with the children go through the skills they are going to need, and make it into a game.

- *We are thinking;*   touch your head.

- *We are looking;*   touch your eyes.

- *We are listening;*   touch your ears.

- *We are speaking;*   touch your mouth.

- *We are concentrating;*   place hands gently together.

Are you engaging?

Explain complex ideas with a light touch, through the use of humour and joyfulness. This approach can decrease significantly any unease that might draw attention away from the innately serious issues that we want everyone to think about. Here are some tips to keep your audience engaged and interested.

Introduce the theme clearly. Make sure the children know, straightaway, that they are about to engage in something that really matters to them in the here and now.

Interact with your audience. Ask questions that either require a show of hands or to which individuals can supply an answer. Using volunteers from all parts of the hall means that the majority of children will attend if only to watch how their classmates behave at the front.

Be a good listener. Model good listening behaviour by leaning forward and reflecting or rephrasing replies. Thank every contributor. A child who is brave enough to speak up and whom you have selected, needs to receive confirmation that they have done their best, even if the answer is irrelevant or silly. A public dismissal of a reply in front of the whole school could mean that that child never dares to speak up again.

Keep praising children for their own listening skills, for example: *I love the way you are all looking at me…I can see at least five listening bodies… I can see lots of hands up which means the room is full of thinking skills… Look at the way those children are concentrating… Thank you so much, children, for making me feel special by the way you are using your skills.*

Vary your voice and behaviour. Children read a lot more from tone of voice and body language than we do. Keep their interest by emphasising this, like an actor on a stage. You don't need to 'ham it up' all the time – this wouldn't be suitable for the times of quiet reflection – but don't be afraid to overact when humour is required. Experience reassures us that you
definitely won't lose any of your authority by acting up a little – in fact, children will warm to you and respect you for being entertaining as well as serious.

And if you do feel nervous, always remember that volunteers and a good supply of props are a great way to spread the load and divert attention while you get into your stride. We remember one occasion when a young, shy teacher went to great lengths to present a puppet show. The teacher was released from her anxieties and the children were captivated.

Are you developing children's skills?

Assemblies offer a unique opportunity to slow down for a moment and reflect quietly. Efficient assembly leaders are able to develop children's thinking skills through appropriate questions and by giving children time to become aware of their thoughts and opinions.

The combination of questioning, thinking and sharing can work wonders and help pupils to develop the depth and quality of their thinking skills.

Sometimes they are asked to think private, personal thoughts and, at others, they reflect together about issues that affect the wider world. These frequent, regular, collective moments of thought help everyone to become more aware of the amazing toolbox they have inside their heads.

New Beginnings

At the beginning of the new school year, you will have spent time making your classroom look bright and ready for the start of a journey that will take your children to new heights of achievement and self-confidence. Everyone is re-energised and hope is in the air. The first assembly reflects this.

Having established a mood of optimism, we continue with a cheerful assembly about the skills of making everyone feel welcome and comfortable. But some children will be nervous as they enter their new class or school, so next, we use a storybook character to help us think about facing up to challenges. This is followed by an assembly about how working together can make life easier for everyone.

It is a good idea to have a toolbox of techniques to keep ourselves calm, so this section concludes with a quiet, reflective assembly in which the children learn a few relaxation techniques to add to their repertoire.

The Things we need

 **Focus**

To refresh children's enthusiasm for learning with each other.

You will need

A selection of essential classroom equipment (wastepaper bin, paintbrushes, rulers, pencils,

library books, computer disc etc), a helpful colleague.

Opening

Tell the children that you have been looking around the school during the holidays, while it was empty and you have decided that it would be a good idea to have a clear out and 'bin' a few things.

Show them the selection of classroom equipment.

Look at your helpful colleague; hold up the computer disc and say: *I think we will clear out all the computer equipment. There would be more space in the school if we did that.*

The helpful colleague must reply: *No, no, you can't do that!*

To which you reply: *Why can't I?*

Your helpful colleague will then list all the reasons why computers are useful in a school – research, printing stories, making books, maths games etc.

Now it is the children's turn and they must do as you and your colleague have done.

1.   Hold up the wastepaper basket and say that you are going to get rid of all the classroom wastepaper baskets.
2.   A volunteer puts their hand up and says: *No, no, you can't do that!*
3.   You reply: *Why can't I?*
4.   The child gives you reasons why wastepaper baskets are indispensable.

Continue in the same way with the other items.

▶ Development

Scratch your head and look as if you are thinking hard. Then say: *Well, maybe we could clear out some of the children.* (Say this with a huge smile so that the children know you are teasing.) *If you cleared out all the children who like to sing, we would have a lot more space.*

Ask the helpful colleague to speak as before: *No, no, you can't do that!*

Now say: **Singing is a wonderful thing. Everyone loves to hear the joyful sound of children singing together. Singing is something that everyone, everywhere, needs to do – it brings us together and makes us feel like a strong community.**

Agree that singing children can stay and think of more categories to 'clear up'. Ask the children to give reasons why these children are essential. Ask for volunteers to put up their hands and speak up for groups like these:

- Children who tidy up the library
- Children who like writing stories
- Children who like art
- Children who are interested in history
- Children who like games
- Children who are very calm

☁ Reflection

As you all have probably guessed, I was just pretending when I made all these silly 'clearing out' suggestions. I was teasing you a little – just because it's so lovely to hear why you all value each other so much. We need all the things that we have in our classrooms but, even more than that, we teachers need all you wonderful children. Every single one of you is important to our school and we simply couldn't do without you.

Let's all join together in a joyful Mexican wave* to show how happy we are that we are all together in our school.

*Mexican wave – Children sit in rows. The child at the right-hand edge of each row raises both arms above their head and then lowers them. The child sitting next to him/her copies this action by raising their arms upward as the person on their right is lowering hers. This continues along each row.

The Meet and Greet Class

**Focus**

To learn how to make someone feel welcome.

You will need

Flipchart and pens.

Opening

Begin with a modified game of hangman.

Draw seven boxes in a line across the flipchart, like this:

Take letter suggestions from the audience. With each unnecessary letter, draw one part of a smiley face near to the boxes.

The word you are building is WELCOME.

Talk about this word by splitting it into two words – 'well' and 'come'.

Ask the children to give you meanings for the word 'well'. This (among other meanings) is a word that we use to say that we feel healthy and happy or that we feel that things in our life are progressing successfully – *'I feel well today, thank you'. 'Yes, our class project is going very well.'*

Now talk about the second word, which means 'movement towards' –*come here, come in, come and join us.*

You can demonstrate this by asking a little group of children to walk towards you one step at a time when you use the word 'come' and beckon them forward.

So, when the two words are put together, you have a big word that means something like:

> *It makes me happy that you are moving towards me.*

▶ Development

Tell the children that making people feel welcome is very important.

Demonstrate how 'meeters and greeters' are taught to welcome people into restaurants and hotels.

Ask two volunteers to come forward and pretend that one of them has just arrived at a hotel in Spain and the other is there to 'meet and greet' them.

Coach the 'meeter and greeter' to do the following things:

- Stand tall. Smile.
- Say hello. Give your name.
- Shake hands. Ask their name.
- Ask some questions: *Did you have a good journey? Do you need any help finding your hotel room? Would you like to have breakfast in your hotel room tomorrow?*

Ask for more volunteers to role-play the following situations:

Arriving at a restaurant – *Would you like a table near the window? Can I get you a glass of water? Shall I fetch the menu now?*

Going into a hat shop – *Hello, my name is Susan, how can I help you? Are you looking for a hat for a particular occasion? Aha, a wedding, please come with me and I will take you to our wedding hat department. Did you have a particular colour in mind?*

☁ Reflection

We all feel nervous when we have to meet new people or go to strange places. Can you remember how you felt when you first came to this school? Perhaps you didn't know anyone and perhaps you were nervous? Perhaps you felt shy? Perhaps you didn't know who to play with at playtime?

Have pre-chosen volunteers to demonstrate how kind children would welcome a shy child in your playground. The kind child can be carrying an imaginary skipping rope. She can ask the new child to turn it with her and a third child could be asked to skip. The children in the hall can be asked if they know any skipping songs to accompany their skipping.

Well, that scene of kindness was wonderful. Making someone feel welcome can make a big difference to how they feel. Show me how friendly you are by sitting up tall and giving me a big smile. That's made me feel much better. Thank you for making such a bright and welcoming start to my day!

I'm a Character - Get Me Out of Here!

🔍 *Focus*

To learn to face up to a challenge.

 *You will need*

The script for a story in which the character faces a challenge but acts bravely. Here we use *Sleeping Beauty* - but you may wish to substitute a story that is better suited to the cultural mix of your school.

💬 *Opening*

Tell the children that sometimes we have to do something that we have never done before and it makes us feel nervous. It might be something like starting school with a new teacher, taking a test, or even going to the dentist. But doing that difficult thing may lead to something good. Today we are going to hear a story about a man who had to decide whether to tackle something difficult.

⏩ *Development*

Ask the children how many of them know the story of Sleeping Beauty. Remind them of the outline of the story using this script

Once upon a time, long ago, a King and Queen lived in a castle. They were very happy because they had just had a beautiful baby girl. She was a little Princess. All the fairies came to the castle to give her a gift. But the last fairy was really a witch in disguise. She said the Princess would prick her finger on a needle and die. The King and Queen were very sad, but one fairy said she could fix it so that the Princess would not die, but fall asleep, until a young Prince would come and wake her up.

Many years passed and everything was OK, until one day, when the Princess had grown up into a beautiful young lady, she did prick her finger. At that moment she fell asleep, and so did everyone else in the castle.

One hundred years went by. In that time, nobody in the castle moved.

Then a Prince came riding by. He heard the story of the sleeping Princess and decided to try to reach her. It was very hard for him to cut his way through the thick trees and sharp brambles that had grown up all around. They bruised him and scratched him. He nearly turned back, but struggled on.

When he got to the castle, it was a scary place. Everything was silent and covered in dust and cobwebs.

The Prince was afraid, but he looked around until he found a bed, where the Princess lay, fast asleep. She was so beautiful he simply had to kiss her!

His kiss woke her up, and at that moment everyone else in the castle woke up. The Prince and Princess fell in love and were married the next day. They lived happily ever after.

The Prince chose to go through the scratchy brambles because he wanted to get into the amazing palace. It was hard and a bit painful but it was worth it in the end.

Sometimes our lives can feel like a patch of brambles. I'm going to read you a list of situations. If you think they are brambly and a bit scary, hold up your hands like this:

Show the children how to make scratchy brambles by holding up their hands and bending their fingers so they look sharp and stiff.

If you think a situation is not scratchy and worrisome, keep your hands very still in your lap.

- Meeting a very big dog on a narrow pavement
- Eating an ice-cream
- Doing a test in spelling or mathematics
- Somebody calling you unkind names
- Stroking a kitten
- Going out to play and finding a huge gorilla in the playground
- Opening a present
- Learning to swim

Refer back to the situation that produced the most scratchy hands and ask for brave volunteers to tell everyone how 'scratchiness' feels inside – wobbly? shaky? butterflies in your tummy? hot and bothered? etc.

⌬Reflection

Sometimes we have to face a challenge. We can choose to tackle it or we can choose to give up. I want you to think about one thing you want to do, but your fear is stopping you. Maybe you feel worried when you see a big dog or maybe you get a fearful feeling when you think about going to the dentist. Or you have a test; or up your hand and answering questions in class; or leaving your mum in the morning. Whatever it is that worries you, I want you to imagine the fear is right in front of you.

Reach out your hand and grab that fear tight in your fist. Hold it hard. Now put your fist behind you, open your hand and let it go. (Mime the action.) Now imagine yourself going forward and achieving what you want to achieve. Now you feel like the Prince; strong and brave. Well done, everyone.

Stone Soup

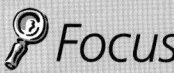 ## Focus

To learn how working together can make life easier for everyone.

You will need

A bag with an ordinary stone inside, some vegetables, a saucepan and some plastic bowls, a big wooden spoon, a tambourine or other musical instrument.

Opening

You can either read this story in the usual way and ask all the children to make appropriate faces as you describe them in the story, or you can choose seven children to come forward and act out the story. One will be the stranger. This child must wait a little way off. The other six children will be villagers. Put the bags of vegetables somewhere close by so they can each pick one up as the story progresses.

Read this story to the children:

The village of Cragmoan was very definitely not a pleasant place to live. It was high up in the mountains of the far north and most of the time there was nothing to see for miles around but icy, swirling snow and nothing to do but stay indoors and hide from the wind and storms.

If the weather at Cragmoan was cold and unfriendly, the people who lived there were even worse. They were cold and unfriendly too and didn't even speak to each other unless they absolutely had to. They never invited each other round for tea and they hid everything they owned in dusty cupboards that were locked not just with one key, but usually with three or four! And if they owned a musical instrument, they played it indoors, all by themselves with the windows closed so that nobody could hear them playing. They were the meanest, most selfish people in the whole world so, as you would expect, they were bored and sad and very lonely.

Tell the six children to sit or stand on their own with their arms tightly across their chests, looking mean and unfriendly.

Development

One day a stranger arrived at the village, carrying a big bag under his arm. He smiled at everybody in a friendly way and didn't seem to mind that not a single person smiled back.

The stranger walks among the villagers, smiling, and the villagers look away.

"You're not welcome here," said one of the villagers, "go away."

All the villagers shoo the stranger away.

"Oh, I will," said the stranger, "but not today. Today I think I will stay and make a lovely bowl of soup and share it with you all."

The villagers watched in amazement as the stranger opened his bag and very carefully removed a rather large, very ordinary-looking stone and a soup pan.

Then he made a fire and fetched some water and very carefully put the stone inside. Then he sat back, stirred the soup and smiled to himself.

Everyone watched as he sniffed the pan and licked his lips happily.

"Oh, I do love stone soup," he said, "though I must admit that it is even better with carrots."

One of the villagers ran off when he heard that and soon came back with some carrots in his hand.

One child must run off and fetch the carrots.

"Just what we needed," said the stranger. "Some potatoes would make it even better though."

Repeat this sentence, changing the name of the vegetable until all the vegetables are in the pot.

When it was ready, the stranger took a pile of bowls from his bag and everyone sat down together and enjoyed the most delicious meal of their lives.

Then the stranger rubbed his tummy and sighed happily before looking into his bag again.
"Aha," he said, "here's my tambourine. I reckon we should have a dancing party. Mind you, a tambourine is not enough to make a dance band. Dancing is so much better with a guitar..."

Can anyone guess what happened next?

Can a very clever child suggest how the village might change from now on?

Who would like to share their thoughts about what the stranger came to teach the villagers?

Ask the children to join hands with the children either side of them and raise their arms if they agree that a particular activity is better if they work together as a team. If they disagree, they must keep their hands in their laps. Read out a list of different activities, such as:

- Playing hopscotch
- Cleaning up after an art lesson
- Reading a book silently
- Playing football
- Concentrating very hard and writing a poem/story
- Keeping the classroom tidy

☁Reflection

Now, ask the children to rub their tummies as if they have just eaten a bowl of the most delicious soup. Then they must take a deep breath and breathe out very slowly and silently. As they sit calmly in their places, say that you will be very pleased to hear that everyone has been working together to make the school happy and successful.

A Feeling of Calm

 *Focus*
To learn relaxation techniques.

 You will need
Nothing.

 *Opening*

Tell the children that you are going to help them understand what it feels like if you are tense. Ask them to screw their hands into a tight ball, hold their teeth tightly together and raise their shoulders. Ask them if they have ever felt tense like that, and what it was that made them feel like it.

Say: *When we are worried, getting tense doesn't help us. So today we are going to learn how to relax, and that will help us when things are difficult.*

I am going to describe to you a very peaceful scene. I want you all to close your eyes and try to imagine you are in this place.

Mmmmm, it's a lovely sunny day.
All the cows are resting in the fields.
The grass is green and soft.
The water in the pond is shiny and smooth.
The butterflies are dancing in the flowers.
I'm lying here watching the clouds.
I am sleepy and happy and warm.

Ask the children how this made them feel. Use prompts if you have to, but encourage them to give you the word 'calm'.

▶️ Development

Ask the children to help you describe other things that make them feel calm. Thank all children for their answers, and reinforce the ones which convey your message.

It is easy to feel calm on a lovely summer day when someone is lying in a field of grass but it can be more difficult to feel calm on other days. Sometimes you feel worried and then it is not easy to be calm. Sometimes you feel nervous and then it is not easy to be calm. Sometimes you are frightened and then it is not easy to be calm.

But there are some simple things that everyone can do to capture that feeling of calm and carry it around with them even if it is rainy and cold.

Ask the children to try out some of the following 'self-calming' techniques:

- The children sit with straight backs, hands resting gently in their laps. Tell them to close their eyes and to think about their breathing. You want them to breathe in a feeling of happiness and then, to breathe out any feelings or thoughts that may be making them unhappy. Next, ask them to picture themselves enjoying a lovely warm summer day, doing things that they really enjoy. Finally, they open their eyes and become aware of the room and the present moment.

- Show the children how to do a temple massage. Gently rub the sides of your eyes and temples with soothing fingertips. Just move the fingers round and round in little circles.

- Stroke the back of each hand. Stroke lightly from the fingertips to the wrist. Do this gently and your hands will soon feel warm and you will feel happy and calm.

- Show everyone how to spend a minute slowing their breathing. Ask them to sit quietly with the hands in their laps, palms upward and count slow breaths – in and out, in and out.

- Tuck in your chin, open your mouth and let your jaw relax. Take four quick breaths through your nose. Twitch your nose like a rabbit. Breathe out through your mouth in a long, smooth sigh. Repeat four times.

- Lead everyone in taking a few deep breaths and ask them to notice their mood. Now show them how to pull their lips into a huge exaggerated smile. Hold the smile for three or four seconds. Repeat.

Ask the children how these activities have made them feel. Which ones worked best?

☁Reflection

Calm is a lovely feeling. We can make it happen whenever we are worried or anxious. It helps us to slow down our bodies and to make us feel relaxed and warm.

Before we go back to our classrooms, we can all practise that deep breathing to put us in a calm frame of mind. Let us all breathe in together slowly to the count of three, 1..2..3.., now breathe out again slowly, 1..2..3.. Now let us stand up very quietly and very calmly make our way back to our classrooms.

Getting On and Falling Out

Making and breaking friendships is a very important part of children's lives, and many of their peer relationships are far from tranquil. Two children may swear everlasting friendship, share secrets and exchange gifts, only to fall out the next day and refuse to even look at one another. This can happen so fast and so frequently that adults find it hard to keep up. The children may understand exactly what's going on but we feel that we need to keep things steady enough to make sure that everyone in the classroom is focused on their work. For this reason, many of the assemblies in this section are designed to investigate ways in which children can work together in a co-operative group.

The first assembly looks at a technique (known as Kaizen) that many people think is the secret of Toyota's success as a car manufacturer. In the following assembly, the world of bees is explored to find out how they keep order in the hive by working together. The section then continues with a look at the different ways in which true friendship can be expressed. This assembly involves a high degree of audience participation that ensures that the children will be working at a level that they all understand.

Then we turn our attention to the damaging effect of selfishness and how this can spoil our relationships with the people around us. The next assembly uses a story about a cat to look at ways in which children can calm down and think when a friend has made them angry.

The section concludes with an active assembly about how we can mend friendships when they are broken.

Kaizen

🔎 *Focus*

To work co-operatively to help a group.

✒️ *You will need*

Flipchart; large picture of a Toyota car for display (try phoning a garage to ask for a poster, or downloading a picture from Google images which you can project onto a whiteboard).

Prepare the class teachers in advance; explain that you will be asking them to come up with a problem/solution (see below).

💬 *Opening*

Display the picture of a Toyota car. See if any children wish to share something they know about this make of car.

Tell the children that Toyota is a very successful manufacturer of cars. Some are made in England, but the company comes from Japan. One of the reasons that Toyota is so successful can be summed up in a Japanese word – kaizen. Write this word on the flipchart:

- **Kai** – means change, or doing something/taking action.
- **Zen** – means good.

Say: *Everyone who works in a Toyota factory is encouraged to suggest changes to make things better. If it works so well for Toyota, it might come in handy in our school. So let's try it out.*

⏩ *Development*

The first thing that has to happen in Kaizen is that someone sees that there is problem.

The second thing is that the person who spots the problem MUST suggest a solution.

No idea is too small. *Kaizen means making small improvements that add together to make the world a much better place.*

Ask some of the teachers present to suggest a real problem and ask for volunteers to come forward and suggest solutions.

For example:

- I need help because people talk too much in the dinner queue and the noise gives me a headache.

Volunteers can use this sentence starter – *Would it help if…?*

- I need help because the library is always left in a muddle.

Would it help if…?

You've all come up with brilliant ideas to help each other. Teamwork is a brilliant support. Let's see if, in just a few minutes, we can create a scene of perfect teamwork.

Ask a group of volunteers to demonstrate how teamwork looks by representing a machine with all of its parts working together. Like this:

The children stand in a line.
The child at the beginning of the line demonstrates a simple movement.
This is copied by each child along the line.
The front child creates more and more movements so that the line is in constant motion.

Reflection

We are people who live and work together and we do this better when we work as a team. Teams need people who put their ideas together and help one another. Wonderful things can happen when we share our ideas. A suggestion may seem small and unimportant but it can make a big difference to other people's lives.

The Bee Team

🔍 Focus

To work co-operatively as part of a group.

📝 You will need

A large drawing of a bee, candles, jar of honey. If you have an interactive whiteboard, log on to Wikipedia, search for European honey bees, and display the section with pictures of the bees and the hive.

💬 Opening

Ask the children if they can name the insect on the picture. Then ask if anyone knows what bees produce, which people use. (Point to the jar of honey and the candles as clues if necessary.) Bees are amazing creatures because they:

- Pollinate flowers so that new plants can grow.
- Make honey that tastes wonderful and is very good for us.
- Make beeswax that is used to make candles and a coating for cheese, dreadlocks and moustache wax (!), and lip-salve.

⏩ Development

Tell the children that on their own bees could not make these things. They have to work together and help each other.

The following information, adapted from Wikipedia, will help you to explain to children how bees work together to make the hive efficient and productive. Adapt it to suit your audience. If you have an interactive whiteboard available, and an internet connection, you could project the section on European honey bees which has pictures of the bees and the combs.

> A colony of honey bees generally contains one breeding female or "queen" each season, and hundreds of males, known as "drones", and some sterile female workers.

Eggs are laid singly in a cell in a wax <u>honeycomb</u>, produced and shaped by the workers. Worker bees produce a special food called royal jelly, which they feed to the larvae. The larvae will spin a <u>cocoon</u> , until emerging as young bees.

Young worker bees clean the hive and feed the larvae. After this, they begin building comb cells. They move to other tasks as they become older, such as receiving nectar and pollen from older bees whose job is to go outside and collect pollen for food. These bees are called foragers. Later still, the young workers leave the hive to become foragers.

Foragers find flowers and suck out the nectar. Then they bring it back to the hive, where worker bees turn it into honey, which bees eat. They store the honey in the honeycomb and seal up the end, leaving it there until they need it.

Workers cooperate to find food and use a pattern of "dancing" (known as the <u>bee dance or waggle dance</u>) to communicate with each other.

Explain to the children that when we all work together, with different jobs to do, it is called team work. Tell them that they are going to work together to make a whole school team.

Tell the children to all stand up. Ask the child at the left end of each row to turn to the person next to them and smile. This continues along the line until every child has a partner. Any odd numbers can be paired up.

Now teach them this clapping sequence:

> *Clap high* (clap above your head) 1, 2, 3, 4
> *Clap low* (clap down by your knees) 1, 2, 3, 4
> *Clap to the right*, 1, 2, 3, 4
> *Clap to the left*, 1, 2, 3, 4
> *Clap with your partner* (both hands together) 1, 2, 3, 4

Repeat this a few times and congratulate the children on their excellent rhythmic teamwork.

Ask them to sit down again.

☁Reflection

There is a way of chanting that is used to keep army cadets working happily as a team. The sergeant calls out the chant with equal stress on each syllable and the cadets repeat what they hear. You could try one like this:

You:	*We're a great team, yes we are.*
Children repeat:	**We're a great team, yes we are.**
You:	*We're a great team, yes we are.*
Children repeat:	**We're a great team, yes we are.**
You:	*Diddly dee and cha cha cha.*
Children repeat:	**Diddly dee and cha cha cha**

Repeat the chant three or more times. Ask the children to think up more verses. Their class can then teach it to the whole assembly.

We are all different and we all have different skills and talents. We can use the things we are good at to work together as a team. Teams are not just about sport. Nearly any job is better tackled together.

The Meaning of Friendship

⌕ Focus

To think about the many ways in which friendship can be expressed.

 You will need

Post-it notes; three pieces of sugar paper fixed securely to the wall; marker pen.

On the day before the assembly, give a Post-it note to each child in one class. Ask them to write on the note one thing that they have done with a friend that day, and to put their name on it. Be sensitive to the fact that some children are loners and may need help to find something they can contribute (you could perhaps give them a 'helping' task to write about). Collect the notes and take them along to assembly. This class should sit at the front.

💬 Opening

Ask all the children what it means to be a friend. Encourage them to find words such as 'loving', 'sharing', 'playing together', 'talking to each other', 'taking care of each other'. Pick three key words (it could be caring/sharing/playing) and write them on the sugar paper, so that you have created three categories with space under each heading to place the Post-it notes. This is your 'wall of friendship'.

⏩ Development

Read out the names of the children who have provided you with the Post-it notes, one by one. Each time you call out a name, that child comes to the front, reads out their activity, and together you decide on which section of the wall to place the Post-it note.

When all of the notes have been placed, you can talk about the many different ways in which we can show our friendship. Ask those children who have not written Post-it notes if they can make any other suggestions.

☺Reflection

Sing this song together, using the tune 'When the Saints Come Marching In'.

We are friends
We are friends,
We are friends at school today.
We are very friendly children
Here at school, this sunny/rainy day.

Footnote:
It would be very helpful if you could involve the whole school in making a 'wall of friendship' display by asking children to draw pictures of friends working and playing together and writing a few sentences about the things friends do together under each picture. This would need to be a whole-school activity supported by your colleagues. This could be done before the assembly to focus everyone's attention (or after it as a follow-up activity).

By the Light of the Moon

 Focus

To understand that friends are generous.

You will need

Two pizza-sized boxes, a bag, wrapping paper, one pizza-sized silver cardboard circle, one pizza-sized silver crescent (like a new moon), sticky tape.

Put the 'new moon' in one of the boxes, wrap it in paper, mark it with a C and hide it in the bag.

Choose a volunteer to help you with the props. This is an opportunity to pick a child who is not usually put into a starring role.

Opening

Tell the children that they are going to hear a fable. This is a made-up story that tells us something about how we should live our lives. The story you are going to them them is about someone who did not want to share.

Long ago, in a world much like our own but also different, the moon was always round and bright and silver in the night sky. Like this:

Child holds up the silver cardboard circle.

This was very useful because travellers were able to find their way by the light of the moon if they needed to travel by night.

But a man who lived in that world was amazingly strong and clever and skilled in magic. He looked at the moon and thought it was beautiful, so beautiful that he wanted it for himself.

So he used his strength and skill and made threads of magic and tied them to the moon. Then he pulled and pulled and the moon was drawn closer and closer until it fell, warm and shining, into his hands.

Then, because he wanted the moon for himself, he put it into a box and carefully wrapped it up and hid it in a bag so no one else could find it.

Ask your volunteer to do this.

Everything went on as usual until the sun set and then the world filled with darkness as if a heavy curtain had been pulled across the sky. Then the world got colder and colder and it began to rain.

Children tap their fingers gently on their knees until you signal them to stop with a clap of your hands.

All the travellers who were out on the roads felt terribly afraid and they called out to whoever had stolen the moon to please, please, put it back so that they could find their way and travel in safety.

The powerful man heard their cries but he put his fingers over his ears and kept the moon hidden in the box.

The next night was as dark as a long winding tunnel and the world turned cold and the rain fell.

Children tap their knees etc.

All the ships at sea went round in circles and bumped into one another and the sailors cried out to whoever had stolen the moon to please, please, put it back so that they could see which way they were going and not get lost on the stormy ocean.

The powerful man heard them but he put his fingers over his ears and kept the moon hidden way in the box.

So it went on for many months and every day when the sun set, the people were filled with fear and stayed at home and waited for the dawn.

Then, one day, the powerful man went on a journey and he wasn't afraid because he had the moon to light his way when the darkness came. He just picked up the bag and happily went on his way, laughing in the bright sunshine. Everything went well for him until the sun set and the world turned black and bleak and stormy. Cold rain began to fall.

Children tap knees etc.

Then he sat down in a puddle and opened the box and this is what he found.

Open the box with the crescent moon in it.

He found that the moon had wasted away in the box. It was just a tiny slither of silver and gave no light at all. For the first time in his life the powerful man felt weak and lost and very afraid. He ran around in a panic and never found his way out of that darkness. So if you hear a moaning sound in the night, don't be afraid, it's only that selfish, silly man wandering around in the dark trying to find his way home.

And the moon? The powerful man's magic changed her forever. Sometimes she grows bigger and rounder and stronger, waxing into a beautiful circle of light, and sometimes she wanes, becoming thinner and sharper and shrinking into a tiny slice of silver that we call the crescent moon.

▶Development

Ask the children if they think this story is true.

It is a good story though, because it tells us something. It is a lesson in a story. Stories that teach us a lesson are called fables, or sometimes parables. In many religions, the holy books tell us stories to show us how we should live our lives.

Would anyone like to have a go at telling us what the lesson in this story might be?

Congratulate all the children for their helpful suggestions.

ᴥReflection

This story shows us that good things should be shared so that everyone can enjoy and use them. People who are strong and clever, but who are selfish and try to keep everything for themselves, often end up unhappy.

To remind us, I would like you to pretend that you have a big biscuit in your hand. Now pretend to break that biscuit in half, and then give half of it to the person sitting next to you. (Mime this for the children, using big exaggerated gestures.) When someone hands you a pretend biscuit, smile and say a big 'Thank you for sharing that with me'.

Blossom the Cat

Focus

To keep calm and overcome feelings of anger.

You will need

A large toy cat or cat puppet (or you could have two children on the stage wearing cat masks to mime the story).

Opening

Read the following story to your children. Use the puppets or ask your two actors to make appropriate actions and noises.

Blossom the cat lived with Pam and Gerry. She had a big fluffy cushion in the living room for when she fancied a sleep and a cat-flap in the back door for when she fancied a walk around the garden. She had two bowls in the kitchen – one for water and the other for food. So, all in all, Blossom was a very happy cat.

That is, until one day, she came in from the garden and found a wire cage in the living room.

It wasn't the cage that startled her. It was what was inside. Can you guess?

Yes, inside the wire cage was a tiny, fluffy, orange-coloured kitten and it was crouching down at the back of the cage looking very scared indeed.

Was Blossom glad to find a little fluffy kitten in her living room? No, she was not. Quite the opposite, Blossom was a very annoyed, very angry cat.

She was so angry that she pushed her tail up in the air and stomped off into the garden. She hissed at the flowers just because they were there.

Then, because anger is a very tiring feeling, she lay down under the shed and fell asleep.

When she woke up, the kitten was still there so Blossom felt very angry all over again. She was so angry that she scratched Pam and Gerry when they tried to stroke her. She sharpened her claws on the sofa. She was so angry that she refused to eat the tin of cat food that Gerry opened for her.

Then, because anger is a very tiring feeling, she lay down in the corner and fell asleep.

When she woke up, the kitten was still there so she went up close and growled and hissed at it. The kitten looked at her with big, frightened eyes and made little mewing noises but Blossom didn't care. She just prowled around the cage looking as mean and big as she could.

Then, because anger is a very tiring feeling, she lay down beside the cage and fell asleep.

When she woke up she was still tired and the kitten was still there. So she just lay where she was and looked at the kitten with sulky, angry eyes.

The more she looked at the fluffy kitten, the more she realised that it was a lonely, frightened little thing. Then Blossom remembered that she had been a kitten once and had felt just the same.

Then she stopped feeling hot and angry and annoyed and started feeling sorry for the new little kitten in the big wire cage.

So she calmed down and started to think about all the things she could show the kitten because she was the boss cat in this house and the kitten had plenty to learn.

She lifted up a soft paw towards the cage and made a kind, soothing sound and waited for Pam to come home so that she and the kitten could get on with the pleasant task of making friends.

Development

Ask the children some questions about the story:

- *Why was Blossom angry?*
- *How did being angry make her feel?*
- *Did being angry do her any good?*
- *Did her anger make the kitten go away?*
- *Did Blossom feel better once she'd calm down? Why?* (Because she could see things more clearly.)

Ask the children to screw up their faces to make them look tense and angry like Blossom the cat. They must do this silently and not look at one another but face you with their tight, angry faces.

Now show them how to relax their faces because if our faces are relaxed, the rest of our bodies will surely follow. Use this script:

- *When we are tense, our jaw gets rigid. Show everyone how they can relax themselves by pressing their tongue on the roof of their mouth, just above the front teeth.*
- *There is a special place on either side of the bridge of the nose. Rub it gently and feel all that tension drift away.*

- *Close your eyes very, very slowly. As your lids get lower, you will feel a sense of wonderful calm waft through your body.*

- *Raise your eyebrows. You will feel tension lift as they rise. You can make this even better by frowning a big worry frown before you raise your brows. Alternatively, you can ask everybody to join you by making a 'surprised' face. This also raises the eyebrows and makes your face feel relaxed.*

⌒Reflection

Sing this song together. Use the tune of 'When Johnny Comes Marching Home'.

> *When Blossom the cat is calm again*
> *Meow, meow,*
> *We'll give a happy cuddle then,*
> *Meow, meow,*
> *We'll tickle her tum*
> *And stroke her fur*
> *And then we'll listen to her purr.*
> *And we'll all feel pleased*
> *That Blossom the cat is calm.*

Sometimes we feel angry and it makes us hot and bothered. When we are angry we sometimes do and say things that are unkind and hurtful. If we do that, then we should say sorry because we know that everyone is much happier when we stay good friends and take care of each other.

Tell everyone to take a deep breath and breathe out slowly as you count to five.

The Way Things Work

> ## 🔎 Focus
> To understand that broken relationships can be mended by being thoughtful.

 You will need

A puppet, a pair of lace-up shoes (which you should be wearing), another member of staff with a piece of string in their pocket (about the same length as a shoelace).

💬 Opening

Walk across the stage with an exaggerated limp. Tell the children that when you were coming into assembly, your shoelace broke. (It could in fact be merely undone.) Show them how the shoe has become loose and slips up and down on your foot. Explain that you cannot walk about like that because you will fall over. Ask for suggestions about what you can do.

Allow time for children's suggestions.

If a child suggests that you should tie a knot, thank them. This is a good suggestion but, unfortunately, the break is a place where a knot wouldn't be helpful.

They may come up with substituting a piece of string. If so, ask if anyone has a piece of string that will do the job. The teacher with the string can then produce it. (If no one suggests it, let the teacher who has the string suggest it.) Lace the string in the shoe and do it up.

Well, that has worked fine for now, and on the way home I can go to the shop and buy a proper new shoelace. That turned out to be quite an easy problem to solve, didn't it? If something is broken, someone may have just the thing you need or maybe you can just buy a new one. But sometimes there are problems that you can't fix with a piece of string.

⏩ Development

Show the children the puppet. We will call it Squeak. Follow this script:

Oh dear, Squeak, you are looking very sad today. Whatever is the matter?

Squeak puts her hands over her eyes and cuddles in close to you.

Could you whisper it in my ear?

Squeak nods to convey 'yes'. Listen to what Squeak has to say.

Well, children, I know what has made Squeak so sad. Would you like to know too?

It goes like this. Squeak's best friend is called Pip. They have been friends for a very long time but yesterday Pip went off and played with Susie and left Squeak all on her own.

That is a problem. What are you going to do about it, Squeak?

Squeak whispers in your ear.

Squeak says she is never, never, no way ever, going to speak to Pip again. Do you think that is a good idea, children?

Take opinions from the audience. A show of hands will be sufficient.

Let's try another plan then, Squeak. What else might you do?

Squeak whispers in your ear.

Squeak says she is going to sit in the cupboard in the dark and not come out until Pip says she is sorry. Do you think that is a good plan, children?

I think Squeak needs a bit of help. Would anyone like to come up and give her some advice?

Let confident children speak for themselves. Allow shy children to whisper in your ear and then speak for them. Help them to use this sentence starter: *'Would it help if...?'*

Ask for audience opinions of the suggestions made.

Now, Squeak, you have heard a lot of useful advice. What do you think you might do to mend your broken friendship with Pip?

Squeak whispers in your ear.

Squeak has been listening very hard and has decided to try ALL your marvellous suggestions.

She wants to thank you very much for being so helpful.

Squeak gives the audience a big wave.

Well done, Squeak. I reckon that you and Pip will be friends again very soon and well done, children, for making such thoughtful and useful suggestions.

ᏪReflection

Sometimes when things break they can be mended with things like glue or string. But when friendships break, we need to stay cool and think about four important words. Those words are: 'Would it help if…?'

Ask all the children to repeat these words with you.

Bullying

Bullying takes many forms and can have a devastating effect on children's self-confidence. It is vital that we nip in the bud all forms of bullying in our classrooms and schools.

There is a children's rhyme that asserts that 'sticks and stones may break my bones but names will never hurt me'. Unfortunately, this simply isn't true. Each of us can remember put-downs and sarcastic remarks that still make us smart years after they actually happened.

The following assembly emphasises the importance of 'boost-ups' to bolster feelings of self-esteem, and encourages children to be kind and helpful to each other. We have tried to help your children by making the message visual as well as verbal.

Would You Rather...?

 **Focus**

To explore how 'boost-ups' and 'put-downs' make us feel.

You will need

A table, two vases, five big flowers and five dry old twigs, two large sheets of thin white paper.

Opening

Tell the children that you are going to tell them a story about a boy called Solomon.

Lay the flowers and twigs on the table beside the two vases.

Choose two children to come to the front.

One child (child A) is in charge of the flowers.
The other child (B) is in charge of the twigs.

Tell the children that each time something kind or helpful is said to Solomon, child A will put a flower in the vase.

Whenever something unkind or hurtful is said to Solomon, child B will put a dry old twig in the other vase.

Use the following script:

Solomon Brown was eager to get to school on Tuesday morning. He brushed his teeth especially well and put gel on is hair to make it look spiky and shiny. Then he went downstairs, singing a song in the best way he could.

"Stop that awful racket," said his brother. "You sound like a frog with a wasp in its throat and you're giving me a headache."

Child B puts a twig in the vase.

His sister looked at his hair.

"You are just soooo embarrassing. You look like a hedgehog in a thunderstorm," she said. "Don't you dare walk anywhere near me on the way to school."

42

Child B puts a twig in the vase.

"It's the choosing day for the concert," whispered Solomon. "I'm just trying to look my best."

Solomon's mum gave him a little hug.

"Take no notice, Solly," she said. "I think you look lovely and I'm sure Mrs Sumner will be pleased that you've made so much effort. You know all the songs already."

Child A puts a flower in the vase.

By the time he got to school, Solomon was starting to worry about his hair. Mary Jane came running up.

"Wow, Solly, you look special. You look just like a film star or something."

Child A puts a flower in the vase.

The first lesson was about telling the time. Solomon tried to concentrate and work quickly but he wrote T I M instead of T I M E. Joseph Brown looked over his shoulder and whispered, "Inky, stinky, Solomon can't spell." And walked off, laughing.

Child B puts a twig in the vase.

Mrs Green came over to see what was going on. She looked at his work.

"Good lad, Solomon," she said. "All your answers are right. Now you can read it through and check that you're spelling 'time' with an e and it will be perfect. Well done."

Child A puts a flower in the vase.

Then they all went out to play. Rory Frost wouldn't pick Solomon to play football because he said he didn't want 'smelly boys with sticky-up jelly in their heads' on the pitch.

Child B puts a twig in the vase.

So Solomon walked off and Joseph Brown followed him, chanting, "What's the tim, smelly jelly boy," over and over again.

Child B puts a twig in the vase.

 Luckily, just when Solomon couldn't stand it any more, Mr Peterson came up and told Joseph not to be so rude.

"Take no notice, Solomon," he said. "By the way, I saw your painting on the corridor wall. It is a lovely bright painting. Well done, lad."

Child A puts a flower in the vase.

Solomon said thank you for the compliment and went to the quiet area for a sit down. Then Tony Scrivener came and sat down next to him.

"Are you going to try for a part in the concert?" he asked. "You're a great singer and I reckon you'll get a good part."

Child A puts a flower in the vase.

"Yes," replied Solomon. "I am. And you?"

"Sure thing," said Tony. "We could go together."

"OK," said Solomon. "See you there then."

And can you guess what happened?

Yes, Tony and Solomon went to the concert try-out and they both got a part. In fact, they got the part of the Terribly Tuneful Twins and sang three songs together, on their own, at the front of the stage, with all the school watching, and the teachers and mums and dads.

And they did it really well and everybody clapped.

At the end of the concert, Solomon and Tony were given a very special job. Can you guess what it was?

Well, I'll tell you.

They had to present Mrs Sumner with a big bouquet of flowers to thank her for putting on

such a great concert and teaching her star singers to perform so outstandingly well.

And twigs? No, there wasn't a twig in sight on that very special day.

Development

Wrap the two 'bouquets' in the pieces of paper.

Ask the audience which they would rather receive – a bunch of kind, helpful flowers or a bundle of hurtful, unkind, dry old twigs?

Explain the words 'put-down' - words that make us feel down and miserable. Say that these are never helpful. What we need are 'boost-ups' that make us feel stronger and pleased to be who we are.

Remind the children of the Golden Rule:

We are kind and helpful – we don't hurt anybody's feelings

Tell the children that you are going to put the bunch of flowers in a prominent place somewhere in the school (e.g. outside the canteen near the main door) so that everyone can see them and remember to think about the importance of boost-ups.

Take the bundle of twigs, break them and put them in the bin as a symbolic gesture to show everyone that 'put-downs' have no place in your setting.

⌲Reflection

When people call us names or put us down, we feel small and hurt. When people say kind things, we feel strong and happy. We must always remember that we have a choice – we can say things in a kind way or we can say things in a hurtful way. We must always choose to do things in a kind way and never be bullies with our words.

Now I want everyone to hold out their arms towards me and give me a thumbs-down. All together, say 'I won't' (mime the thumbs-down and frown in an exaggerated way). Now smile, show me a thumbs-up and say the words, 'I will' to show that you will always try to say supportive, kind and helpful things to one another.

Ask your colleagues to join in and give a thumbs-up if the children are doing this task in a sensible way and a thumbs-down if they are being silly.

Going for Goals

Some children find it easy to set goals and work towards them. They know that motivation requires persistence, and they keep going through thick and thin. Other children seem confused and lacking in the sense of direction and stamina that they need to pull them through. The assemblies in this section are designed to remind children about the things we all need to do in order to be successful.

The first assembly looks at how covering up the truth only makes matters worse. The second is concerned with the concept of persistence. We can learn a lot from sand. It takes thousands of years to become just the right size to make a good beach. If it takes that long to make sand, who are we to complain about the time it takes to reach our goals?

The next assembly looks at someone who overcame many rejections before she found fame and fortune as an author. This is followed by an assembly that uses the amazing growing properties of grass as an example of how children can bounce back after experiencing difficulties or setbacks.

The section continues with a look at the importance of proceeding one step at a time in order to achieve our goals. The final assembly explores the need to put everything together in a neat package, along with some hard work and effort, in order to attain success.

Trouble with Tumble

Focus

To take responsibility for our actions.

You will need

A dirty coffee mug, a puppet or large cuddly toy, flipchart. Write the following statements on separate sheets:

> **Be reliable: when you agree to do something, you do it.**
> **Do it yourself: don't make others do what you are supposed to do.**
> **Be honest: don't blame other people or make excuses.**

Opening

Introduce the puppet or cuddly toy. Say that her/his name is Tumble and that s/he is very soft and lovely BUT s/he sometimes has a problem with telling the truth.

Sit Tumble on your lap and use the following script. Make sure that Tumble looks suitably ashamed/surprised/happy as the story unfolds.

Tumble, I've brought you into school today to meet the children. Say hello, please.

Children, Tumble is usually my friend. Sometimes I ask him to do little jobs for me when I am at school. This is what happened yesterday.

Tumble, before I left for work, I asked you to wash up my coffee mug. I remember that you said, yes, you would do that for me. Do you remember saying yes?'

(Tumble nods in agreement.)

But look at this mug. It still has coffee in it so you didn't do what I asked, did you?'

That means that you didn't do what you said you would do. That means that you didn't act responsibly."

Go to the flipchart and point out the statement:

Be reliable: when you agree to do something, you do it.

And there's another thing. I asked you to brush up the crumbs under the table. When I came home that job was done and I was pleased but then Mrs Sharp from next door came round and she said that she'd nipped in during the morning and you asked her to brush them up and she did. So you didn't do that job did you! You made Mrs Sharp do it. That's not taking responsibility.

Go to the flipchart and point out the statement:

Do it yourself: don't make others do what you are supposed to do.

Now, you'd better explain this to me, Tumble. I found some pieces of scrunched-up paper on the table. How did they get there?

Tumble makes excuses and blames Mrs Sharp for the scrunched-up paper.

Now that's very naughty, Tumble. I know that Mrs Sharp would never waste paper. I think you have forgotten the third thing about being a responsible person.

Go to the flipchart and point out the statement:

Be honest: don't blame other people or make excuses.

Well, children, Tumble hasn't been a very good puppet recently, has s/he, but s/he has shown us three very important things about how to be responsible people.

Development

Make Tumble look very sad and ashamed for a moment, and then show him starting to whisper in your ear.

Oh Tumble, you are saying that Mrs Sharp has a headache and you would like to go and make her a cup of tea and that would make up for blaming her about the paper?

Turn to the children.

I think that would be a very good thing for Tumble to do, don't you? So, Tumble has one more thing to add to the list about how to be a responsible person. This is definitely the best rule of all.

Go to the flipchart and write:

Take responsibility for the things you do well, and feel pleased with yourself!

Now I think that although Tumble did not behave very well while I was out, he has decided to change and behave responsibly now, so let's all give him a clap.

☁Reflection

We have the power to make other people's lives easier or harder. We can be helpful or unhelpful. We can take responsibility and see things through or we can be careless and lazy. We should do what we can to help other people by keeping our promises and helping out whenever we can.

Sand

Focus

To wait for what we want and be persistent.

You will need

A rock or large pebble, small pebbles, a handful of gravel, tray of damp sand, bucket and spade, medi-wipe to clean hands.

Opening

Tell the children that sometimes we have to wait for things to happen. Show them the tray of damp sand.

Invite one child to come forward and make a sandcastle.

Ask: *Does anyone know of any ways we use sand?* For example:

- Sandpaper – to make wood smooth.
- Sandbags – to stop flood water going into houses.
- Sand in an egg timer.
- If you mix sand with soda and limestone you can make glass.
- Landing area of long jump.

So sand is both useful and enjoyable.

Development

Ask: *Who knows how sand is made?*

Invite one child to come up and hold the big, heavy, pebble.

Yes, sand starts out as a big stone like this.

What might happen to turn this big pebble into a million grains of sand?

Well, it happens like this: hot and cold – sunshine and frost and ice – break up big rocks and make them split and become smaller rocks.

Rivers, glaciers and the sea, churn the pebbles and make them rub against each other and polish and polish them so that all their rough edges are smoothed away. The broken bits of rock get smaller and smaller.

Ask the children to mime the action by rolling their hands around each other in big circles.

Next, show the gravel.

The rubbing and breaking go on and on until, eventually, the gravel is worn so small and fine that it becomes sand, and we have miles and miles of sand on the beach to make sandcastles with.

Ask the children to mime the action by rolling their hands around each other in small circles.

How long do you think it takes to make a beach full of sand?

Take answers from the children and stress that it takes a very, very long time for a rock to turn into sand.

Ask them to mime the action by rubbing their thumbs against their fingers.

The weather has to keep changing from hot to cold and the stones have to be rubbed together for years and years before a beach of sand can be made.

So, there is something very important we can learn from sand and I want you to remember this important thing every time you look at the sand tray or play on a beach. The lesson is this: sometimes it can take a very long time indeed to make something which is beautiful and useful and which we enjoy.

Explain that there are lots of things in this life which are going to take us a long time to achieve. Ask if any of the children have something they would like to achieve which will take a long time. Invite volunteers to say what their goal is.

⌬Reflection

It takes a long, long time to make a beach of sand. It can take a long time for us to learn how to do the things that we want to do. But if we are patient when the going gets tough and if we have faith in ourselves and keep going and if we are prepared to work hard, we will reach our goals in the end.

If At First You Don't Succeed

Focus

To be persistent and not give up easily.

 You will need

Copies of Harry Potter books and Harry Potter paraphernalia or posters; a doll's pram, a table and chair, a writing pad and a large envelope. (You can mime the JK Rowling character yourself, or ask one of the older girls to do it.)

During the week before the assembly, ask your colleagues to nominate a few children who have struggled to overcome obstacles. Prepare some certificates or badges for these children. These do not need to be academically successful children but will be children who are real ' triers' who have pushed themselves to do something they find difficult – someone who has learned to swim, a child whose handwriting has improved because they practised hard at home, etc

Opening

Invite the children to share their opinions about the Harry Potter books and films.

Say: *JK Rowling is a good example of someone who wanted to get something done, but found it wasn't easy. But she did not give up. Her biography is on her official website and here is how she came to write and publish the Harry Potter books:*

One day JK was on a train going to London. There was a problem and the train was delayed for hours. JK was stuck on the train and to pass the time she began to imagine a story. The character of Harry Potter just popped into her head, and she began to dream up more and more things about him.
(Mime sitting in the train and thinking.)

Unfortunately, JK did not have a pen and paper with her, so she could not write down the wonderful story which was beginning to form in her mind. Instead, she had to try to remember it all. As soon as she got home, she began writing it down.
(Mime walking up to the table, sit down and start writing furiously.)

But lots of other things were happening in her life at that time which stopped her getting the story finished. It was only when she decided to get a job as a teacher that she realised she had better try to get it completed, because once she was teaching, she might not have time.

Also, JK had little baby daughter called Jessica, and she had to look after her. So she wrote in every spare moment. As soon as Jessica fell asleep, she would push her in her pushchair down to the café, and sit there writing. Then when Jessica went to bed, JK would write long into the night.
(Get up and push the pram backwards and forwards. Then sit down and start writing again.)

Eventually *The Philosopher's Stone* was finished. She sent it off to companies who might publish it for her. She tried and tried, but they kept sending it back saying they did not want to publish it.
(Mime opening an envelope, looking upset at its content, then sitting down to write again.)

It took a year to find someone who wanted to take it.

JK kept trying. She could easily have just sat on that train and looked out of the window and got cross because the train was late. But she didn't.

She could easily have just forgotten about the story in her head, but although it must have been late when she got home, she started writing it down.

She could easily have stopped writing when she had a daughter to look after and she had to go out and get a job – but she worked even harder to get it finished.

She could have given up when no one seemed interested in her book, but she kept on trying. And you all know what happened after that. JK went on to write seven Harry Potter books – and the books and films are famous all over the world.

▶ Development

Congratulate those children in your school who have persisted and have finally succeeded.

Give out the certificates or badges that you have prepared and hold a parade of honour for these children.

Ask for volunteers to share their ambitions. It is a good idea to prepare a few children so that they have little speeches ready. Ask them to come forward and talk about the things they know they will have to do in order to be successful. Congratulate them on their clear thinking and ambition.

Reflection

JK Rowling was greatly encouraged by her friend, Sean, because he had faith in her abilities. Without Sean's kind words she might never have written her books. Think about things where you have persisted and not given up. Think of anyone who has encouraged you. Think how you can encourage your friends and give them confidence.

Grass Just Keeps on Growing

🔍 Focus

To be resilient and, if we run into difficulties, be prepared to try again.

 You will need

A picture with grass (e.g. a park, a garden, or field); any potted plant with shoots near the top of the stem; a pair of garden shears.

💬 Opening

Show the children the picture of a patch of grass.

Ask for volunteers to contribute information about grass – where it can be found, how it is used by humans and animals etc. Thank each child for their contribution.

Tell the children that there is a very big difference between grass and most other plants. Grass does a very special and interesting thing – which you are going to ask some children to demonstrate.

Call a group of children to come forward and pretend to be grass – standing straight and tall with arms in the air.

Pretend to use the pair of garden shears to cut the grass. (Children sink to the floor and curl up.)

Ask: *What does the grass do when it has been mowed?*

Yes, it grows back up again! (Tell children to grow again.)

What happens when a herd of cows comes along and eats all the grass in the field? (Children repeat being cut and growing again.)

Ask the volunteers to return to their seats.

Why does this cutting and growing keep happening? Because there is a very interesting and special thing about grass that makes it different from other plants.

Show the children the potted plant.

Most plants grow from the top – they put out shoots at the tip of their branches (demonstrate) *and if you cut them off at the bottom they will probably die*

But grass is different. Grass grows up from its base very close to the ground. It doesn't grow from the tips of its leaves, but from the bottom. This means that however many times it is cut or eaten, it can just start growing again. Over and over again it gets cut back; but that doesn't stop the grass – it just keeps on growing.

▶Development

Ask the children if they can think of anything that we might learn from grass.

Take suggestions and comment positively on any that suggest the concept of 'bouncing back'.

State that there is a word that is very useful when we think about what we can learn from grass. That word is 'resilience'. It means that we pick ourselves up after setbacks and carry on, even when the going gets tough.

For example, someone might do badly in a spelling test and then decides to try harder for the next one and do much better. Can the children make up other examples of classroom resilience?

Ask the children to remind themselves about the grass by holding up the fingers of one hand and pretending they are blades of grass (demonstrate), then making the fingers of the other hand into scissors. Use the 'scissors' to cut the 'grass' and then make the grass grow again.

Reflection

Sometimes things can go wrong and we can feel like giving up. Those are the times when we need to take a good look at a field of grass and remember that we can bounce back just like grass does.

Whiz-quiz

 Focus

To look at how role models set and achieve goals.

 You will need

A whiz-quiz chair (an ordinary chair covered with a large piece of material), some willing colleagues and two confident children.

💬 Opening

Give the children the definition of a whiz: *An expert; someone who is very skilled at something – e.g. a computer whiz.*

Show them the 'whiz-quiz' chair.

Invite the headteacher to come forward and sit in the whiz-quiz chair.

Ask him/her questions about how to become a whiz headteacher. (If you are the headteacher, then ask your secretary about how to become a whiz secretary. In fact, as long as they have been prepared, you can ask any member of staff.)

Mrs Sumner, you are our headteacher. Being a headteacher is a very important job and we would be very interested to know how you became such a whiz.

Let's start at the beginning. What were you like at junior school? Did you work hard and listen to your teachers?

When you started out on your career, did you become a headteacher straight away? What did you do before you were a headteacher?

Thank Mrs Sumner for telling everyone how to become a whiz.

⏩ Development

Now ask other helpful colleagues to tell the children about their whizziness – how they became good at football coaching, how they became a lunchtime supervisor, what they did so that they could play the piano in assembly, how they learned all about computers and so on.

Invite the audience to ask questions of the person sitting in the whiz-quiz chair. Alternatively, ask some previously prepared children to come forward and sit in the whiz-quiz chair and answer questions about their hobbies and interests.

You could also ask your colleagues to pretend to be someone famous and to answer questions about what this person did to become a whiz.

The important thing is to stay on the subject of explaining what is involved in becoming a whiz – hard work, perseverance, goal setting etc.

☁*Reflection*

Each and every one of us has it in us to become a whiz. Every whiz that there ever was started out being just ordinary and then worked very hard to whizify themselves by practising and keeping going when things got tough.

Now we are going to celebrate all our achievements with a big whiz. When I lift up my arms, I want you all to smile and say:

'I'm a whizzzzzzzz!'.

You must stop as soon as my arms come back down to my sides. Are you ready…?

Now I want you all to take a deep breath and hold it for a second before letting it out very, very slowly as I count to five.

Putting It All Together

> ##  Focus
> To find out what it takes to set and achieve goals.

✍ You will need

A large coat, gloves, hats and scarf. Optional: popular dance music and player, dancing shoes, ribbons, mirror, and other things that a dancer might need. (Alternatively, you may wish to choose other goals and will need the equipment suitable for these, such as pens/notebooks for a writer, or a football kit.) A chair for Mary Jane.

💬 Opening

Explain that today's assembly is about setting and achieving goals.

Ask for three confident volunteers to come to the front. Tell them that you want them, one at a time, to put on the coat, hat, gloves and scarf; run to the hall door and back again. Explain that it is their goal is do this as quickly as possible.

Ask the audience to help you time each child by counting with you – very quietly.

Give each volunteer a go at reaching this goal. If there is a clear winner, ask him/her to talk about the things that made the goal easy to reach. Give prompts if you need to and repeat any useful replies: 'I concentrated', 'I decided on a plan' and so on.

If everyone reached the goal in about the same time, you can ask them about their strategies as a group.

⏩ Development

Have ready all the things that are needed to be a successful dancer. (You could just read out the following script as a story if you can't find all the equipment, but acting out the scenario is more engaging for the audience.)

Choose two confident children to come forward and enact this script. (You may wish to choose one talented dancer and talk to her before the assembly so that she knows what she has to do.) Alternatively, you might like to use a puppet.

Mary Jane came home very excited and told her mum that there was going to be a dance competition at school. She told her mum that she was going to enter the competition and, what is more, she intended to win.

Then she sat down and thought about it. The more she thought, the more clearly she could see that she wouldn't win unless she had a really good pair of dancing shoes. So she asked her mum to buy her some.

The next day, after school, Mary Jane came home and found a lovely pair of dancing shoes waiting for her on the table. She was really pleased, so she put them on and sat down on her chair and thought about just how wonderful it would be to dance in her new shoes at the competition.

Then she realised that shoes wouldn't be enough and she could clearly see that she wouldn't win unless she had a lovely dancing dress. So she asked her mum to buy her one.

The next day, after school, Mary Jane came home and found a lovely dancing dress on the table. She was so pleased that she hugged it and then she sat down on her chair and dreamed about being a rich and famous dancer like the ones she'd seen on the television. And after she'd dreamed for a while she could clearly see that she wouldn't win if she didn't have some sparkly things to go in her hair. So she asked her mum to buy her some.

The next day, after school, Mary Jane came home and found a bag full of lovely sparkly hair bands and clips waiting for her on the table. She was very pleased and she tried them on, every single one. Then she went and got a mirror and sat down on her chair and looked at her reflection until bedtime.

The next day was the day of the competition so Mary Jane put her shoes and her dress and her hair things in a bag and rushed off to school feeling very happy.

Then, after her lessons were over she went to the hall and waited for her turn to dance. The teacher put on the dance music and told Mary Jane to begin.

Put on the music and play it while Mary Jane stands still. Turn the music off and look at the audience.

Recap all the things that Mary Jane has done to get ready for the competition. Ask: *Which piece of 'getting ready' has she forgotten? Yes, she has forgotten a very important part of achieving our goals. She forgot to put in some hard work. She forgot to think of a dance and practise it.*

Then, say that the person next to you is definitely not Mary Jane, she is (use her real name) and she never forgets to practise her dancing.

Put the music on again and let her dance to loud applause.

⌣Reflection

Hard work and effort don't always feel like much fun but they are well worth the effort. Even if they are very talented, people still need to practise and work on their skills. Practising and training improves our skills and are the only ways to get really good at something. Practice and training make us feel confident and sure or ourselves. So the effort is always worth it

Good To Be Me

Not so long ago, school children tended to be sorted into three groups – the good, the naughty and the lazy! Thankfully, we are now much better informed and know that some children face a great many obstacles in their journey to become successful learners. We also know that how children **feel** about themselves has a dramatic effect on their proficiency as learners. We try to ensure that every child feels good and valued as a member of our school community.

In the first assembly in this section, we learn about Mr Dickson, who helped his clumsy wife and became a very rich man as a result. Then we move on to celebrate the small successes that make children feel good about themselves, before looking at ways in which questions can help us to work and behave more productively.

The next two assemblies look at how worries can easily get out of proportion and we help children find ways to make them shrink.

Finally, there is an assembly about strategies for dealing with the angry feelings that get us into trouble if we don't control them.

We all need to feel good about ourselves and we all need to feel wanted and valued so this section contains invaluable scripts that can be used whenever you feel that children need a lift.

Saving Mrs Dickson

🔎 Focus

To know that something special can come out of something ordinary.

 You will need

Three bandage strips (and safety pins to fasten them), a packet of adhesive plasters, a roll of adhesive tape, white kitchen roll, achievement stickers.

You can bring the story to life with other props, such as a plastic plate, plastic knife, an apron for Mrs Dickson and a bow tie or man's hat for Mr Dickson.

💬 Opening

Tell the children that you don't need to be special or famous to do something to be proud of.

Ask for two confident volunteers to come to the front and be Mr and Mrs Dickson, from America. Help them put on the bow tie (or man's hat) and the apron. Now read out the following script as the children enact the story.

Mr and Mrs Dickson were two very ordinary people. They lived in an ordinary house and lived ordinary lives. They weren't good at anything in particular. In fact, Mrs Dickson was rather bad at one thing – she was a terrible cook.

When she chopped onions, she cut her finger and Mr Dickson had to bandage it for her. (Act this out.)

When she fried onions, she got in a mess and burned her hand. Mr Dickson had to bandage it for her. (Act this out using the other hand.)

When she put the onions on the plate she dropped it and hurt her leg and Mr Dickson had to bandage it for her. (Act this out.)

In the end, both of them were worn out and Mrs Dickson was covered in bandages.

Mr Dickson had to go to work every day and he worried about Mrs Dickson, all alone in the kitchen getting covered with cuts and bruises.

So he thought and thought and in the end he came up with an idea.

He decided to make a kind of bandage that Mrs Dickson could put on all by herself.

He found some sticky tape. (Hold up the adhesive tape.)

And he found some clean, white material. (Hold up the kitchen roll.)

He cut the pieces of material and stuck them on the tape. He had to try for a long time before he got it right. (Have some untidy ones ready and, dramatically, throw them away. Have some good ones ready and hold them up, looking pleased.)

He gave them to Mrs Dickson and showed her how to use them. (Put the 'plasters' all over Mr Dickson.)

She was very pleased and told him that he had made a really good invention.

And he had. He had invented plasters. (Hold up some real ones.)

Ask the children how they think Mr Dickson might feel when he realised how clever he had been.

Of course, he felt pleased because, even though he was ordinary, he had done something to be proud of.

What did Mr Dickson do that helped him to be successful and proud of himself? He cared about his wife, he thought hard, he persevered and didn't give up, he used his imagination.

▶️Development

Announce that you have made some very special 'Mr Dickson' awards. Say that anyone who receives them can feel very proud.

Give out some achievement stickers to deserving children and/or ask children to nominate one another for special commendation.

Make this a joyful event and hand out the awards with a flourish.

🗨Reflection

We don't all have to be famous. Feeling proud of yourself is something that anyone can achieve. The important thing to remember is that feeling proud of yourself is a very good feeling, and a good feeling is the best reward of all for all the hard work you have all been doing.

Good To Be Us

 **Focus**

To feel that it really is 'good to be me'.

You will need

A selection of four big pictures – for instance, a giraffe, a car, an ocean, an eagle, a footballer (but almost any large picture will do!).

A list of ten children who have made an effort recently or who need a boost. (Ask your colleagues for suggestions.)

Ten cards with the letters **b, d, e, e, g, m, o, o, o, t** – one letter for each card.

Calming music, e.g. *Cello Suite No 1 in G Major* by J S Bach, or a CD of nature's sounds.

Opening

Hold up a picture (we are using the giraffe) and say something like this:

I've always liked the idea of being a giraffe because

- *They have long necks and can eat leaves that other animals can't reach.*
- *They have long legs and can run fast.*
- *They are gentle and don't hurt other animals.*

*Yes, it must **feel** good to be a giraffe.*

Then ask for volunteers to come forward and follow your example by explaining why it must feel good to be the subject of your other pictures.

Development

One at a time, ask the ten chosen children to come forward and make positive statements about them without being too overpowering. Like this:

Jonah's teacher has been telling me just how hard he has been working lately. Well done, Jonah.

Give Jonah one of the cards to hold.

Continue in this way until all ten children are standing at the front holding a card.

Ask them to stand in a row and hold up their cards.

Ask if anyone in the audience would like to come forward and unscramble the letters to make a sentence.

Give prompts if necessary:

- There are four words in the sentence
- Three of the words are only two letters long

When the sentence – **good to be me** – is found, ask the audience to give everyone a clap.

⟳*Reflection*

Ask the children to repeat each line of this rhyme and then say it together.

> *It might be good to be a giraffe*
> *A dragon or a bee.*
> *It might be good to be a car*
> *Or a spaceship*
> *Or the sea.*
>
> *But most of all,*
> *Best of all,*
> *Definitelyyyyyyyyyyyyyyy,*
> *It is good   (thumbs up)*
> *It is good   (thumbs up)*
> *It is good   (thumbs up)*
> *To be me.   (point to self)*

Ask the children to sit very still with their hands in their laps, listen to the music and silently think about all the things they have to feel good about.

The Three Whys

 ## Focus

To ask questions that help us clarify our thinking and improve our behaviour.

You will need

Two statements written on separate pieces of paper, such as **'Felt pens come in many colours'** and **'Football is a great game'**.

Opening

Say: *If we ask questions, it can help us to sort out our ideas. We can use the 'three whys' system. All we need to do is ask the question 'why?' three times, and the answers will help us to get things clearer in our mind. Let's try it. I need two volunteers to help me. Who will come and try the 'three whys'?*

Child 1 reads the statement: *Felt pens come in many colours.*
Child 2 asks: *Why?*

Child 1 replies: *Because we need a lot of colours.*
Child 2 asks: *Why?*

Child 1 replies: *Because then we can make the grass green and the sky blue.*
Child 2 asks: *Why?*

Child 1 replies: *Because that makes our pictures look bright.*

(Other answers are fine!)

Repeat with the second statement.

Development

Explain that you are going to use the 'three whys' to help us to understand how we can deal with problems.

Invite six pairs of volunteers to come forward and, one by one, try out the 'three whys' with these statements:

- It is useful to look at people when you talk to them.
- It is useful to put your hand up in class.
- Everyone has the right to say 'no' when they need to.
- It is useful to tell people how you feel.
- Getting angry can make it hard to solve problems.

Give prompts if necessary.

Ask the children to share what they have learned from this exercise and commend them for their clear thinking.

⏣Reflection

When we have a problem, or are feeling confused and off balance, it is a good idea to stop and think and ask ourselves some questions because questions lead to answers and answers are what we are all looking for.

Let's end by each of us drawing a big question mark in the air like this (show the children a large picture of a question mark or draw one in the air – remembering to turn round so they don't have to reverse your action) *and as we draw it say to ourselves 'Why, Why, Why'.*

So, when you feel that things are getting difficult, ask yourself some questions and see if you can find ways to make things easier and more straightforward.

The Worry Wheel

Focus

To learn that listening is important if we want to help.

You will need

Make a worry wheel by cutting out a large circle of card. Divide the circle into eight segments. Find the middle and fix a strip of card to make the pointer. You can fix it with a split pin or a mapping pin so that it is able to move round and round.

Put a 'worry buster' on each one, like this:

- Get more sleep
- Keep it in your pencil case
- Work harder
- Put your name on it
- Take more exercise
- Tell them to go away
- Smile at her
- Tell them to go away

Make some cards of possible worries (keep to school worries). For example:

- My handwriting isn't very good
- I worry about playtime
- I worry about writing stories
- I worry that people will laugh at my hair
- I worry because I can't kick a ball straight
- I worry that other people think I am not very clever
- I worry that people will say my shoes are scruffy.

Put these in a bag or envelope.

Opening

Introduce the 'worry wheel' by excitedly telling the children that you have made a wonderful new invention that will help them with their worries.

Invite a volunteer to come to the front and take a worry card out of the envelope/bag.

Read the 'worry' and ask the child to spin the wheel. Read out the 'worry buster' statement on which the pointer has stopped.

Ask the child if the worry wheel has been helpful.

Say: *No? Oh well, we can try it with another child.*

Try it a couple more times and then stop and look confused.

⏩Development

Tell the children that the worry wheel doesn't seem to be working very successfully. What could be wrong with it?

When children suggest a fault, ask them this question: *What could you do that the wheel doesn't seem to be able to do?*

For example, if the child says, 'The answers don't fit the worry', you could reply: *So you're saying that the worry wheel isn't listening properly? In other words, you have to be able to **listen** well to help someone with their worry.*

If the child says, 'The pointer spins round very quickly and just stops at random', you can reply: *So does that mean that the wheel isn't thinking before it decides on an answer? In other words, you need to **think** carefully before you give your advice.*

When you have enough answers, you can ask for a list of things that people can do that a worry wheel can't do, such as:

- Stop and listen carefully
- Ask more questions
- Get some background information
- Give thoughtful replies
- Give respectful replies

Say: *There seem to be a great many reasons why human beings are better at helping people with their worries – a worry wheel will never be as useful as a good friend.*

Thank the children for their wise contributions.

☁Reflection

Listen carefully to your friends when they are unhappy or anxious. By thinking about what they are saying and working with them to find a way out of their troubles, we can help them to find ways of being happier and more calm.

Get the whole assembly to say together: *The best question to ask is always: Would it help if…?*

Treasure Hunt

 Focus

To help someone with a worry.

You will need

Treasure hunt cards (see below). These will contain two things:
- a common school-based worry (ask your class to write some for you – they don't need to put their name on the suggestion)
- directions to the next card.

For example:

I am worried about people laughing at me.
The next card is under a teacher's chair.

I am worried that no one will play with me.
The next card is behind a curtain.

Opening

The first card will only give instructions – not a worry. The first volunteer reads it and sets off to find the first worry card.

When the child has found the first worry card, they read out the top section only. Ask for helpful suggestions. You can use a sentence starter: *Would it help if… (you just ignore people who laugh and think about how silly they are being?)*

The child then chooses their favourite suggestion and gives the card to the person who offered the suggestion.

This child then uses the clues on the second part of the card to find the next worry. This continues until all the cards have been located.

▶️Development

Ask the children how they feel when they get worried. How does a worry feel inside their heads? Teach them this little rhyme:

When I worry,
I get all in a flurry.
Till I feel as hot and bubbly
As a big prawn curry.

Let them do some worried hand flapping in front of their faces as they recite this rhyme.

Add some more lines to the rhyme:

That's when I tell myself to STOP. (Clap hands)
And cool down. (Slowly put hands on laps)
And think. (Put one finger on forehead)
And blow them away. (Put hands on either side of mouth, breathe out slowly)

💭Reflection

When we get hot and bothered it is hard to think clearly. Help us to cool down and think carefully. Help us to remember that worries will get bigger and bigger if we let them, but we can make them smaller if we choose to take control and blow them away.

The Van That Didn't Count to Ten

 Focus

To learn how to deal with feelings of anger.

You will need

If possible, before the assembly, ask a child to draw a picture of a futuristic van. Enlarge the drawing onto A3 paper and make four copies. Colour in three of the copies – pink, purple, red.

Opening

Tell the children that you are going to tell them a story. Commend the child who has done the drawing which you are going to show them. Show the first drawing and explain that the story is about a van that might be made in the future – a very clever van. But although the van knows how to steer itself, it doesn't know how to control its feelings.

Way ahead in the future, in the year 3017, an inventor invented a big white van that didn't need a driver. All you had to do was fill it up with whatever you wanted delivered, tell it where you wanted it to go by typing the address on its dashboard computer, and off it went.

This was a wonderful invention because it saved a lot of van drivers the lonely job of driving through the night to deliver things to far away places.

Show the children the picture of the smart white van.

Everything went very well until someone put 100 boxes of fish in the van and sent it to the north of Scotland to deliver them.

The thing that nobody realised was that the smell of fish upset all the complicated wires and switches inside the engine and made the van very irritable and cross.

So as the van drove along the long road to Scotland it got pinker and pinker and more and more cross.

Show the picture of the pink van.

What should the van have done?

Yes, it should have stopped. It should have stopped in a lay-by and pulled itself together. But it didn't. It just kept on going, hot and bothered.

Then it started to rain. The van didn't like rain because rain makes mud and the mud splashed up and got into the engine and made the van feel twitchy and scratchy.

Ask the children to mime the sound of the rain by drumming on their knees with their fingers.

So the van got more and more angry. Its engine heated up and the van turned purple and started driving all over the road because it was in such a bad mood that it stopped looking where it was going.

Show the picture of the purple van.

What should the van have done?

Yes, it should have stopped. It should have called in at a service station and cooled its engine down by sitting quietly for a while. And then it should have refreshed itself by putting fresh clean water into its engine and maybe had a lovely cool shower in the car wash.

Ask the children to mime filling up the water tank.

But it didn't. It just kept on driving up the road, weaving all over the place, with nasty grumbly noises coming out of its engine.

Then it stopped raining and the sun came out. The sun got brighter and brighter and all the soggy mud inside the van's engine dried up and felt prickly and gritty on its pins and pistons.

Ask the children to mime the sun with their hands, making circular movements.

This was too much for the van. The fish was smelling and the engine was getting hotter and hotter and more and more angry. The lovely white van started to get redder and redder as it went along.

What should the van have done?

Yes, it should have stopped. It should have sheltered under a tree, in the shade, and counted to ten, or a hundred, or however long it took to calm down and make itself feel better.

Show the picture of the red van. Ask the children to make fanning movements with their hands.

But it didn't. It just kept racing along, faster and faster, not looking where it was going and not thinking about what it was doing.

Until... well, I expect you can guess what happened next.

The van got more and more angry, and red and careless, and then, quite suddenly, it exploded.

Ask the children to make an exploding movement with their hands.

You could hear the banging and crashing of that explosion a hundred miles away as the van broke into a thousand pieces that flew up into the air, bright red with heat and anger. Then all the pieces landed again looking grey and charred and very, very tired.

What a sight it was. There were bits and pieces of the van lying all over the place in an untidy muddle. Bits of engine got mixed up with fish and the smell was horrible. It took 17 men five days to clean up the mess.

And it never would have happened if the smart white van had calmed itself down when it had the chance.

▶Development

Tell the children that sometimes we can be like the white van. But we have a choice, just as the van had a choice. We can notice when we are starting to feel angry and we can stop it right there and then.

Ask: *What are the things we can do to stop ourselves getting out of control with anger?*

Take suggestions from the assembly and write these on the flipchart.

⌂Reflection

Remember that anger is something that we can all control. We just need to learn to stop and give ourselves time to calm down. Counting to ten can make a big difference to our lives because those ten precious seconds give our body time to cool down. Then our brain can start thinking clearly again.

Let us all count to ten in a very quiet whisper.

Now we will all breathe in very quietly and slowly let the breath out while I count to five.

Relationships

This section opens with an examination of the need to be fair and treat each other well. In the first assembly a clever inventor makes a plan to undo the damage that a jealous man has done. The second develops this theme by looking at strategies each of us can use to make sure that life is as fair as possible for everyone around us.

The next assembly shows the importance of showing others that they are appreciated and valued; this is followed by a look at the undesirable repercussions of telling lies and how they have the effect of only making matters worse.

Then we look at ways to salvage damaged relationships and learn how to say sorry in a way that really works.

The final assembly offers children a straightforward way to make others feel secure and wanted. It tells the story of a poor man and a king. Each has a wife but one wife is much happier than the other. Which husband knows the secret of good relationships and which one doesn't? Your children will be interested in the answer!

The Sky House

 Focus

To use positive thinking to change an unfair situation.

 You will need

Nothing.

 Opening

Ask the children whether they have ever been blamed for something and felt that it was just NOT FAIR. Tell them that today they are going to hear about a man who was treated unfairly, and they will discover what he was able to do about it.

Read out the following script.

Augustus Pine was a good man. He never told lies, or said hurtful things or trod on snails just to hear that crunching noise. He was clever too – and he was especially clever at inventing things. In fact, he worked as an inventor for the Sultan of Dubitoo.

Most people liked him because he was good and many people admired him because he was an inventor; but one man, Archie Sour, hated him. Archie was mean and moody and he was jealous of all the wonderful things that Augustus had invented.

So Archie went to the Sultan and told him a story. He said that Augustus was a show-off and a big-head. He told the Sultan that Augustus Pine was going around town bragging that he could build a house in the sky. And not only that, he could build that house in just five days.

Now, what do you think about that? Yes, it was mean and unkind and very definitely NOT FAIR.

But the Sultan wasn't very smart and he fell for all of Archie's lies. He went to see Augustus and said, "No ifs or buts, Augustus. I won't take no for an answer. I demand that you build me a house in the sky and you have just five days to do it in. If you fail I will be very angry indeed."

Then he walked away.

Well, what do you think about that? Yes, it was mean and unkind and very definitely NOT FAIR.

Augustus Pine sat down in his chair and thought for a long time. What do you think he was thinking about? Yes, he was trying to think of a way to solve his problem.

Then Augustus Pine got up and went into his office. What do you think he was doing? Yes, he was making a plan to get himself out of difficulty.

Then he went to the market place and bought rolls and rolls of the finest silk and a needle and thread and some scissors and a great many balls of string.

What do you think he was doing? No, I don't know either but, whatever it was, it kept him busy for the next four days and nights.

On the fifth day, he went to the park and carefully made a fire. Then he unfolded his silk invention and held it over the hot air and smoke. The silk filled up with hot air and lifted up, into the sky.

And, just at that moment, the Sultan looked out of his window and what do you think he saw?

Yes, he saw an amazing hot air balloon rising up towards the clouds. It was made in the shape of a house with yellow walls and white windows and a bright red roof.

It was the first hot air balloon that was ever invented and it was a wonderful sight.

▶ Development

So that is how Augustus Pine changed an unfair situation into a triumph. Who can tell me how he did it?

- He stayed calm.
- He thought carefully and wisely.
- He came up with a plan.
- He took action and made his plan happen.
- And, he did it all without hurting anyone else or getting his own back.

If there is time, ask the children if they wish to share examples of how an unfair situation was changed.

Recap the ways in which Augustus behaved and point out that these behaviours are helpful, whereas getting angry or bitter can stop us being able to put things right.

Reflection

Life is not always fair. In fact, sometimes, life can feel mean and unkind and very decidedly 'not fair'. But it is up to us to think positively and try to turn a bad experience into a good one.

We can use our thinking skills to make our world a better place for everyone.

The Smelly Sock Game

 *Focus*

To consider how we can treat people equally and with fairness.

You will need

Two large cardboard cut-out socks (one blue, one red); three envelopes, each containing a description of an enjoyable task.

Confer with colleagues before the assembly and choose three tasks that the children would enjoy doing. For example:

- help the secretary for half an hour
- be first in the queue for lunch on Tuesday and Wednesday
- help Mrs Brow in the library on Monday and Friday lunchtimes.

Opening

Ask the children whether they have ever played in a game and felt that it wasn't really fair, because they didn't have a chance of winning. Tell them that today they are going to take a look at how they might do things in a better way so that everyone gets a fair chance.

Say: *We are going to start with a game called Smelly Socks.* Give the cardboard cut-out socks to two children in different parts of the assembly. Ask them to pass the socks from child to child while you all chant the following rhyme. When you get to 'mmmm', the two children holding the socks must stand up.

Short socks,
Long socks,
Old socks,
Smelly socks,
Urrgh (hold your nose)

Yellow socks,
Red socks,
Blue socks,
New socks,
mmmmm.

The children who are holding the socks when you say 'mmmm' must come to the front. Tell them that they going to help you.

Repeat this until six children are standing at the front. Put 'blue sock' children in one group and 'red sock' children in another.

Ask the assembly if this was a fair way to pick volunteers. Ask them to give reasons for their answers. For example:

- It was fair because everyone had a chance.
- It was unfair because shy children who don't like coming to the front were selected.

▶️Development

Select one child from each of the two groups. Say that you are in charge and you are giving one child an envelope with something nice in it and the other child nothing at all.

Hand one child an envelope and ask/help them to read out their surprise.

Ask the rest of the children: *Do you think this is a fair thing to do? Why not?* Take reasons.

Then ask: *How could we make it more fair?* Take suggestions from the children. For example, they might suggest that the time with the secretary could be shared so that each child helps her for 15 minutes.

Choose or vote for a fair solution.

Next, choose two more children, one from each group. Take an envelope and put it behind your back. Ask them to choose a hand. One child will win and the other will be faced with an empty hand. Read out the surprise.

Ask: *Was this is this a fair way to do things?* (Each child has a 50/50 chance of winning. One child is disappointed.)

Ask for suggestions about what you should do in this situation. For example, you could divide the 'prize' and give each child a chance to be first in the queue at lunchtime.

Tell them you have a third surprise envelope. This time the two children are going to share their surprise. Ask them to stand very close together with their nearest arms around each other's back and open the envelope, each using their free arm. This takes teamwork and is a display of solidarity.

💭Reflection

It is important to treat everyone as equally and as fairly as we can. We should never leave people out on purpose and we should give everyone a chance. If we are lucky and get something good, we should think about others who were not so lucky and share when we can.

Let the Sunshine In

Focus

To learn the importance of appreciating others.

You will need

A large yellow circle of stiff paper or card for a sun, with a smiley face on it. Approximately eight strips of card which will form the sun's rays; a marker pen; plastic adhesive sheets; a recording of 'Here Comes The Sun' by The Beatles to play as the children enter the hall.

Opening

Have the smiley sun pinned up on display, but without the 'rays'.
Ask the children to guess why the sun is smiling.

The sun feels good because everyone is pleased to see it and says nice things about it. Do you know what we call it when someone says nice things about someone else? We call it 'giving a compliment'.

Can anyone think of a compliment that you could say to a friend?

Take suggestions. When a child volunteers something appropriate, write it on one of the strips of card (e.g. looking nice, being friendly, helping, being good at something, telling the truth). As you write each one, stick the strips of card around the sun, like rays.

When you have put on eight rays, stop and point out that the sun makes us feel warm, bright and cheerful. That's how we feel when someone gives us a compliment.

Development

Have the smiley sun pinned up on display, but without the 'rays'.
Ask the children to guess why the sun is smiling?

The sun feels good because everyone is pleased to see it and says nice things about it. Do you know what we call it when someone says nice things about someone else? We call it 'giving a compliment'.

Can anyone think of something you could say to a friend, which would be a compliment?

Take suggestions. When a child volunteers something appropriate, write it on one of the strips of card (e.g. looking nice, being friendly, helping, being good at something, telling the truth) As you write each one, stick them up around the sun, like rays.

When you have put on eight rays, stop and point out that the sun makes us feel warm, bright and cheerful. That's how we feel when someone gives us a compliment.

Now I want each of you to turn to the person next to you and give them a nice compliment.

When the children have had a few minutes to do this, check that everyone received a compliment. If anyone got left out, give them one yourself.

Ask the children how it made them feel to receive a compliment.

⌐*Reflection*

We all need to hear that we are loved, liked and appreciated. Teachers and parents like compliments too, so remember to thank them for all the good things they do for us.

If the children sit in rows and are calm and peaceable, you might like to allow them to lean forward and gently rub in a circular movement, the back of the person sitting in front of them so that each child (except the back row! Perhaps the staff could do this for them?) can feel something like the warmth of the sun for a few moments.

A Jumble of Lies

 Focus

To learn the Golden Rule 'We are honest: we don't cover up the truth'.

You will need

A poster (get one from a travel agency or project a picture from Google images onto a whiteboard), flipchart and pen.

Opening

Show the children the poster and make some statements about it. Some will be true, some untrue, e.g. the sky is blue/black; there is a banana/boat on the water, etc.

Ask for a show of hands to show that children consider your statements to be true or untrue.

Development

I wonder if any of you have ever told a lie to get yourself out of trouble? The trouble with telling lies is that they make our messes and mistakes get bigger and bigger instead of helping them to go way.

Give the children a scenario, like this, and ask for suggestions from the audience.

One day, a boy called Seth went home and told his mum that he'd got 10 out of 10 in his spelling test when, really, he'd only got 1 right.

What would happen then?
(His mum would expect him to do just as well next week.)

What would happen then?
(He would have to lie again.)

The next week, he lost his spelling list on the way home. His mum wanted to see the list so he told her that a bigger boy had taken it away from him, screwed it up and put it in the bin.

His mum was very angry and asked him the bully's name. Seth was a bit stuck and in the end he made a name up and said, "Billy".

What might happen next?
(His mum would go and see Seth's teacher and Billy might get into trouble.)

The next week, Seth said that his teacher had forgotten to give his class any spellings.

What might happen then?

The next week, Seth said that he had learned his spellings at lunchtime and didn't need to do them at home.

What would happen if his mum came into school and talked to the teacher about how well he was doing?

What should he have done?

What will he have to do now?

Did you like the story?

I need to be sure that you all remember what this story is about so I'm going to test you with a riddle.

What does Father Christmas say, usually three times?

Take suggestions from the audience and thank the child who answers 'Ho, ho, ho.'

Write 'ho' on the flipchart.

What does a bird live in?

Take suggestions from the floor and thank the child who answers 'a nest.'

Write 'nest' on the flipchart.

If we put those two words together, we can make a new word. It sounds different. Who can read the new word?

Thank the child who answers 'honest'.

'Honest' is an important word about something we must always try to be.

Encourage everyone to repeat the Golden Rule:

We are honest; we don't cover up the truth.

⟲Reflection

It is better to tell the truth even when we are afraid. Although that may be difficult for us, it will not be so bad as getting found out after we have told a lot of big lies, and we will have a better chance to put things right.

The Squashed Cake

Focus

To face up to mistakes, say sorry and make amends.

You will need

A cheap cake in a cardboard box, a carrier bag, a willing colleague, a flipchart.

Prepare your colleague for what she/he will need to do. Put the boxed cake into the carrier bag.

Opening

Stand up and welcome the children to the assembly.

Your colleague must then come to the front and say that she needs to go out of the hall for a moment. She asks if you would please look after her carrier bag while she is gone. Then she puts the carrier bag on your seat.

Complete the welcome and sit down – on the carrier bag.

Jump up and hold up the bag. Open it and take out the squashed box. Open the box and show the children the squashed cake.

Say: *Oh dear, I've squashed Mrs Brown's cake. What to you think I should do now?*

Take suggestions from the children and accept that you will need to say sorry.

Tell the children that you will need to practise saying sorry before Mrs Brown comes back and ask if they will help you to get it right. Like this:

I could say, *'I'm sorry but it's your fault for leaving the bag on my seat.'* Would that help?

Prompt them to give you the answer – no, because then you'd be blaming Mrs Brown for the squashed cake.

I could say, *'I'm sorry but it's only a small cake. It's not as if it's a birthday cake or anything.'* Would that help?

Prompt them to give the answer – no, because that will make her think that you don't care.

I could say, 'I'm sorry but it would only have made you put on weight. Cake is really not that good for you.' Would that help?

Prompt them to give the answer – no, because she would think that was rather rude.

I could write a note and ask Mr Green to give it to her. Would that help?

Prompt the children to say that it is much better to say sorry face-to-face.

⏩Development

Sum up by saying that there seem to be rather a lot of ways of saying sorry that don't work too well. So what is the best way to say sorry?

List these ideas on the flipchart:

- Say sorry face-to-face
- Take responsibility
- Don't try to blame the other person
- Show that you care and realise that the other person is upset
- Say sorry as soon as you can
- Mean what you say

Mrs Brown can then return to the hall and you can make your apology. Tell Mrs Brown that you would like to make another cake for her, to make amends.
Mrs Brown might even say that she will make the squashed cake into a trifle. (If you are feeling lively, you may even decide to make a trifle and bring it in to the next assembly with a flourish!)

💭Reflection

Saying sorry isn't always an easy thing to do. Saying sorry isn't always enough. We need to DO something to make amends. We have to feel sorry in our hearts. Try to think about how the other person must be feeling and be ready to do everything you can to make them feel happy again.

Tail Soup

 **Focus**

To understand why people might feel lonely or sad.

✍ You will need

A flipchart and marker pen. Optional: a saucepan containing bits of string to look like tails.

Prepare three or four confident children to have a good joke ready.

💬 Opening

Show the children two words that sound the same but are spelled differently – tale and tail. Talk about these two words so that everyone is clear about their different meanings. Tell the children that sometimes problems can arise because people get the words confused.

Now read the following story:

Once upon a time, far away and long ago, a king and queen lived in a palace. The king was always very busy doing the things that kings do and he never seemed to find the time to enjoy life with his wife. When they married she was young and beautiful but as the years went by she got thinner and thinner and sadder and sadder.

The king did what he could and asked his cooks to make her lovely dinners but they didn't seem to do her any good and she kept on sitting by herself and looking weary and tired.

Then, one day, the king was out in his carriage when he saw a poor man and his wife. He looked at the wife and thought how healthy and well she looked. So he asked the man, "How is it that your wife looks so fine and plump?"

The poor man smiled at the king and said, "The answer is simple, your Majesty. Every evening, when I get home from work, I feed her with tales - long tales, short tales, funny tales and strange tales."

The king didn't stop to hear more. He didn't stop and ask if the poor man meant tales and stories, or tails from animals. He heard the word, 'tail' and rushed home and dashed straight into the kitchen. He told the cooks to make his wife dinners from tails.

The cooks looked surprised but they didn't want to argue with the king so they made as many dinners as they could. The made oxtail soup and pig tail pie. They made goat tail pizza and cow tail stew. They even made dinners from squirrel tails and lion tails and fish tail tarts. In the end they had a whole recipe book of dinners you can make from animal tails.

(Pick up the saucepan, look in it , stir it round, pull out some of the 'tails', and look as if you are going to be sick.)

And did the queen get better? No, she did not. She wasn't very fond of tail food and grew thinner and sicker as the days went by.

The king wanted a plump, happy wife so he decided on another plan. He sacked all of his cooks and went to the poor man's house and demanded that the queen should come to stay for a while to see if the poor man's cooking suited her any better.

Every evening, the poor man would come home from work and he would sit down and tell stories to his wife and the queen. He told tales about the things he had seen and thought during the day. He would tell them funny tales and interesting tales and tales people had told him in the market square. Then he would get out his guitar and sing them songs and entertain them with jokes and amuse them so that they were never bored. Then, the next day, he would go to work and think of new tales to tell them when he got home and they would spend the day doing housework and smiling about the tales he had told the night before.

Then, one day, the king came to the house to see how his wife was getting on. When he saw her he was amazed to see how beautiful and happy she looked. "Well", he said, "the poor man must have a very special way of cooking tails for you to be looking so cheerful and lively."

"Cooking?" said the queen. "He doesn't cook tails, he tells them. And when he tells them, he makes me feel wanted and joyful and content."

The king looked at her for a long time while he thought about what a fool he had been.

"Aha", he said, "now I understand. And what is more, I have a very funny tale to tell you about a stupid king and a clever poor man. Perhaps you would like to come home with me now and I will tell it to you this evening, after dinner."

So the queen went back to the palace and stayed happy and cheerful and full of laughter. And the king often invited the poor man and his wife round for tea. The poor man always took his guitar along in case they felt like a song.

⏩Development

Choose a volunteer to come forward and be the sad, lonely queen. All the audience are the courtiers.

The selected children must now come forward and tell their jokes. If she loved it, then she claps loudly; if she quite liked them, she claps lightly. The courtiers copy her lead each time.

Now ask her how these jokes made her feel.

💬Reflection

Sometimes each and every one of us feels lonely or sad. When we see someone who looks that way, there are many things that we can do to help him or her feel better. We can be generous and gentle and give each other interesting things to think about or kind words to cheer them up.

Changes

Change happens: that's one fact of life that we can't change. But we can find ways to cope with the unexpected or unwelcome things that happen and force us to readjust our lives to accommodate them.

The first assembly investigates how unexpected change makes us feel and how it can throw us into a state of uncertainty. This is followed by an assembly that explores ways in which we can change our behaviour in order to become more effective learners.

Then we look at how each of us needs to become increasingly autonomous. American Independence Day falls at just the right time to fit the theme and is used as the stimulus for this assembly.

The next assembly explores the need to modify our behaviour when things don't work in the way we want them to, in order to change our lives for the better. This is followed by an assembly that uses the joyful occasion of Midsummer's Day to understand the importance of having a positive attitude.

The section concludes with an assembly that looks at unwelcome change. This can be a tricky issue for many children who have little or no control about the events in their lives, but it has been sensitively approached in a simple scenario that uses a bag of apples and a potato as props.

Only Tea-sing

 Focus

To cope with unexpected change.

📝 You will need

A large box of dog biscuits, carrot sticks or tasty biscuits, plastic sandwich bag, shopping bag, table, tablecloth, plates, flipchart.

Carefully open the dog biscuit box and empty it out. Put the carrot sticks or tasty biscuits into the plastic bag and put the bag in the dog biscuit box. Reseal it and put it in your shopping bag.

💬 Opening

Ask: *Who enjoys a tea party?* Invite a few volunteers to come to the front and have tea with you.

When they are sitting down, ask them how they are feeling (physical, emotional feelings and thoughts).

Say that you have some unusual things for tea. Bring out the dog biscuits and show everyone the box.

Ask the volunteers how they are feeling now! (Physical, emotional feelings and thoughts.)

Open the dog biscuit box and show everyone what is inside.

While the volunteers are quietly enjoying their tea, talk to everyone about what has just been going on. Tell them that you arranged the surprise biscuits because you wanted to investigate how we cope with the unexpected.

⏩ Development

Ask the children to think about they cope with unexpected changes. You may need to prompt with some examples:

- You arrive at school and find out that your best friend is away.
- Your mum usually drives you to school but her car won't start.
- You get home and find that your whole street has no electricity.
- Your television won't work.

Collect the coping strategies and write them on the flipchart. If the children are reluctant or unable to give suggestions, you can prompt them with questions such as: *Would it help if... you played with someone else? Would it help if.... you found some games to play with?*

Thank everyone for their contribution. Using your list, bring out some coping strategies which focus on changing your behaviour (adapting) to cope with the new situation.

Ask everyone to remember that important question – all say it together just to help the children to remember it: *Would it help if...?*

✑Reflection

Sometimes things don't turn out to be as we were expecting, and then we get a nasty surprise. But we can use our thinking skills to help us make the best of a new situation.

Training Matters

 Focus

To find out how to become more effective learners.

You will need

Two small tables, two chairs, one larger table, flipchart; the equipment listed below, plus a range of other small classroom resources.

Opening

Before the assembly, you will need to write a task on the flipchart. For instance:

Today's task

What to do	You will need
Draw a square	Paper, pencil, ruler
Draw three shapes on it	Shape templates
Colour them in	Felt pens
Cut it out	Scissors
Mount it on card	Card, glue
Copy your favourite poem on the back	Book of poems
Punch a hole in the corner and put string through the hole	Hole punch, string
Hang it up in the reading corner	Drawing pin

Then you need to fill the big table with the necessary equipment – and a lot more besides.

Choose two confident volunteers before the assembly and prepare them for their different roles.

97

💬Opening

Ask the two volunteers to come forward and sit at the two smaller tables.

Show everyone the task on the flipchart.

Child A must go to the table and grab as many things as he can and carry them back to his table.

Child B must take only paper, pencil and ruler and arrange them neatly on his table.

Ask the assembly to guess which pupil will do better at the task. Ask for reasons to support choices. Congratulate anyone who notices that child B is clearly better organised.

Child A must now sort himself out by taking unnecessary things back to the big table.

Then child A gets on with his work, taking what he needs for each stage of the task and keeping his table clear and tidy.

Child B sits at his table and stops concentrating – he plays with his shoe, stares out of the window, waves to his friends etc.

Ask the assembly to guess which pupil will do better at the task now. Ask for reasons to support choices. Congratulate any child who uses the word 'concentration'.

⏩Development

Talk about why learning is so vital to us all.

Point out that learning is something that we can work on to improve. Just as athletes train so that they can run faster, so we can train ourselves to be better learners.

Ask everyone to think what they can do to train themselves to be better learners.

Ask if anyone would share what they have decided. Praise any child who does this.

💭Reflection

We can all be better learners. We can be organised in the way we approach the tasks we need to do. We can look after the things we need and use them in a way that will keep them safe and unbroken. We can work quietly so that we can concentrate and not stop others from working.

Independence Day

> ## 🔍 Focus
> To work towards independence in our learning.

📝 You will need

A wall map to show where America is (optional: American flag, picnic set, baseball bat, American music) flipchart.

💬 Opening

Show the children where the USA is on the map and find out what they know about it. Talk about Independence Day:

In America they have a big festival on 4 July. It is to celebrate the day in 1776 when America became a country which could rule itself instead of being ruled by another country. The festival is called Independence Day. 'Independence' means you can do things for yourself. People parade in the streets, have barbecues with their friends, go to baseball games and let off fireworks.

The Americans made this day into a special day because they were so pleased that they could do things for themselves and they celebrate it every year.

⏩ Development

Say: *As you are growing up, it is important for you to learn to be independent too. This means you will be able to:*

- *do things for yourself*
- *make your own decisions*
- *do things without asking adults for help.*

Ask for volunteers to come forward and show things that they can do independently (adapt these to suit the age and ability of your children).

When you started school, you couldn't write your own names and needed help. Who would like to come and show us how they can write their name independently?

Who can spell the word _____ (cat, difference, musical etc) *without needing any help?*

When you first came to school, you all needed counters to help you do your maths. Who would like to come to the front and show us their skill at mental maths?

Ask for a show of hands for some non-academic things which children can do for themselves (adapt questions for different age groups):

- Put up your hand if you can do up your own shoes.
- Who can write their own name?
- Who can swim across the pool?
- Who can recite the alphabet?
- Who can recite the alphabet backwards?
- Who can ride a bike?
- Who can draw a picture of an elephant?
- Who can wiggle their ears?

Pick out one or two children who raise their hands each time and ask them if they like the feeling of being independent.

☁*Reflection*

We have all come a long way in our lives. We can do things today that we couldn't do yesterday. We are all moving forward and becoming more and more independent. We can all feel proud of the progress we have already made in our lives.

Close your eyes for a moment and think of one thing you would like to do on your own. Now think of one thing that you have learned to do recently.

Now all join together and do a whole school Mexican wave* to celebrate so many things each of us can do this year that we couldn't do last year.

*Mexican wave – Children sit in rows. The child at the right-hand edge of each row raises both arms above their head and then lowers them. The child sitting next to him/her copies this action by raising their arms upward as the person on their right is lowering hers. This continues along each row.

Felt Pens

 Focus

To recognise that sometimes we need to change our behaviour.

 You will need

Some felt tips for hand-writing, colouring pens, board markers, flipchart. A puppet.

🗨 Opening

Hold up a packet of ordinary felt pens. Ask the children to suggest different ways in which we use this type of felt pen. Demonstrate on the flipchart (or ask volunteers to come up and do this).

These are great felt pens for doing pictures in a notebook. The people who invented them must have been very clever but I don't think these pens will be so good for handwriting. Perhaps I should tell the people who make pens about this?

Well, actually, someone must have told them already, and they must have thought about the problem and then they took action and made some changes because now they have made these handwriting pens.

Handwriting pens have a thinner, firmer tip, which makes them good for handwriting.

Hold one up and demonstrate on the flipchart.

But when I am writing here (point to flipchart) I need to write very big letters so that you can all see what I'm writing and these handwriting pens are no good for that.

Yes, you've guessed: the people who make felt pens thought about that problem and then they took action and made some changes.

And here is what they made – a marker pen. They are bigger and have a wide felt tip so that you can all see what I am writing.

Demonstrate.

⏩ Development

So, let's think about those clever people who make felt pens. What did they do that was so clever?

Write: **how to make changes**
Well, what did they do first?

Write: **think**
But thinking wasn't enough. Next they had to…?

Write: **act**
Did they give up when things got difficult? No, they kept going until everyone was happy with their changes.

Write: **keep going**

Then offer the children some behavioural scenarios that need to change in your school. Use a puppet to demonstrate this script:

Ellie was always getting too upset. When she was upset, she would storm out of the classroom and sit at the end of the corridor and refuse to move.

What could she do to change her behaviour for the better?

Refer to the sequence list on the flipchart and take suggestions from the children. For instance:

- She could think about how much she disrupts the classroom,
- She could think about the trouble she is causing for her teacher.
- She could decide to stay in the classroom and sit in the quiet corner when she is upset – that would be a change for the better.
- She could remember all the things she has learned about how to stay calm.

Collect these suggestions on the flipchart. Let Ellie thank the children for their contributions.

Do this calming exercise together:

- Ask the children to stand up
- Tell them that they are each holding a huge bottle that is just a little bit taller than they are.
- Ask them to hold the heavy bottle and to reach up to the big screw top.
- The top is stuck and they need to struggle to remove it. Encourage them to act out the strenuous stretching activity. Give instructions like: "Push harder, try to turn the big stopper."
- Talk them through turning the cap very slowly by saying things like, "Slowly, slowly, the top is getting looser. Looser and looser, good, keep going."
- Then ask the children to put the imaginary top on the floor.
- Now wafts of wonderful calming perfume floats out of the bottle and drifts down all over each child, making them feel warm, relaxed and happy.
- Let them feel the calming effect as the perfume gently covers them. What does it smell like? Lavender? Candyfloss? Strawberries? Allow them time to imagine their own soothing perfume.

- Ask the children to breathe in very slowly and deeply so that the calm can seep into their bodies.
- Tell them to feel the warmth of calm as it goes inside and soothe their whole body. Let them take five slow deep breaths and then, gently, ask them to sit down and get ready for the reflection.

Reflection

We all have choices. None of us is stuck. We can all change. If we know our behaviour is not right, we should think about it, decide to act and then we will be able to change our lives for the better. Think if there is anything in your behaviour you would like to change, and if there is, decide what you are going to do to change.

Midsummer's Day

🔍 Focus

To appreciate the power of a positive attitude.

📝 What you need

Happy, summertime music such as 'Oh what a beautiful morning' from Oklahoma or 'Wonderful world' by Louis Armstrong.

💬 Opening

Talk about Midsummer Day:

Midsummer Day is a special day in the middle of the summer. You may have noticed that in the summer, it doesn't get dark until quite late at night. On Midsummer Day, we have the longest day of the year and the shortest night. This is celebrated in many countries around the world.

In France they light bonfires on 24th June and have parties.

In Portugal people eat a special meal of cabbage and potato soup, grilled sardines and red wine.

In Denmark everybody has a day off work.

In Sweden it is a big holiday and people dance round maypoles and eat strawberries.

So, all around the world, it is a day of celebration and joyfulness.

⏭️ Development

Play the happy, summertime music. How does it make the children feel? Does it make them smile and dance?

Tell them that the sun makes us feel like that too. We are happy when the sun shines, and not so happy when it rains.

Point out that we have the power to make every day like Midsummer Day. We can warm up even cold, grey days and we do that by doing one simple thing – we can smile at one another.

Ask the children to make a big frown and hold it while you count to ten. How do they feel at the end of the long grey frown?

Now ask them to make a huge exaggerated smile – raised eyebrows, teeth exposed (it doesn't matter that it is a false smile!). Hold it for a count to ten.

How do the children feel now?

Ask them to suggest times when a simple smile can make things easier and better.

- Going to your new school
- Meeting new people
- When someone is feeling sad and lonely
- When someone is finding their work very difficult
- When they get home in the afternoons
- When mum or dad get home from work

Point out that smiling is something that everybody can get good at. Everyone can decide to smile more and make every day warm and joyful like midsummer.

⌒Reflection

Let us join together to make our school a lovely sunny place. We all know ways to do that. Let us decide right now to make today a wonderful, happy day for everyone by remembering to smile at each other as often as we can.

End the assembly with everyone joining in this song.

If you're happy and you know it, clap your hands.
If you're happy and you know it, clap your hands.
If you're happy and you know it, then your face will surely show it.
If you're happy and you know it, clap your hands.

If you're happy and you know it, wave your hand.
If you're happy and you know it, wave your hand.
If you're happy and you know it, then your face will surely show it.
If you're happy and you know it, wave you hand.

If you're happy and you know it, nod your head…

Who Likes Apples?

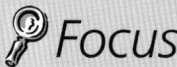 *Focus*

To make the most of an unwelcome change.

 You will need

Three apples of different eating varieties, one potato, paper, flipchart, and another juicy apple hidden in your bag.

Before the assembly, wrap each apple, and the potato, with paper. Mark each wrapper so that you know which variety of apple is inside.

Opening

Ask: *Who likes apples?*

Call one volunteer to the front and give them an apple.

Say: *Mmmm, this apple feels good so I'm giving it to you, Shirleen.*

Ask Shirleen to unwrap the apple. Tell everyone which variety she has received. Ask her to describe it.

Ask Shirleen how she feels about being given a lovely juicy apple. Is she looking forward to eating it? Does it feel good to be given such a lovely apple?

Repeat with the other two eating apples.

Call up a confident volunteer, and give him the wrapped potato.

Ask if he is looking forward to unwrapping his apple.

Let him unwrap the 'apple' and discover that it is a potato.

Ask him how this experience feels. Prompt the word 'disappointed'. Ask him to tell everyone how it felt to be expecting a juicy apple and receive a potato instead. Ask for as much detail of his reaction as possible.

Development

Talk about how all of us, at some time or another, have to cope with disappointment or unwelcome change – just as the last apple turned out to be a potato.

When unwelcome change happens we have to find ways to cope with the disappointment and frustration.

Tell a little story about how this once happened to you (for example, a cancelled holiday, a picnic that couldn't happen because it rained).

Ask for volunteers to give a short example of their own. Ask them how the unwelcome change felt.

As they describe their experience, share some strategies for dealing with these situations. Use the *'Would it help if…'* sentence starter, such as:

Would it help to STOP and calm down and not get into a state?

Would it help if you gave yourself some time to think it over and see that things might not be quite so bad?

Would it help to let out your uncomfortable feelings in a way that doesn't hurt you or anyone else? What ways do you have to do that? You could punch a pillow; sit on your bed for five minutes until you have calmed down; have a cuddle with a grown up, etc.

Collect these insights and write them on the flipchart.

Thank the last volunteer for taking his disappointment so well and reward him for his fortitude. Then give him a welcome surprise by handing him the juicy apple you have hidden in your bag.

⌒ﾟReflection

The taste of juicy apples is something that most of us look forward to. As potatoes are meant to be cooked and cannot be eaten raw, it was not a good experience for ___ (name child) when he found he'd been given a potato instead of an apple. He had a bit of a disappointment, didn't he?

He felt much better when I gave him the lovely apple. I was able to take his disappointment away. But, unfortunately, that can't always be done and everybody has to face a disappointment sooner or later.

The good ideas that you have come up with today will help us through difficult times. And if our friends have some disappointment, let's think about ways we can help them to feel more cheerful, because receiving love and friendship will always help us get over a disappointment.

It would be fun to give each child a segment of apple as they leave the hall – and one big apple for each adult. If possible, make friends with your local grocer!

Quality Circle Time has been developed by Jenny Mosley over the past 20 years as a whole-school approach to enhancing self-esteem, developing positive behaviour and relationships within the school community. For more information visit our website www.circle-time.co.uk

Also available:
Step-by-Step Guide to Circle Time for SEAL
by Jenny Mosley

This is a first-stop introduction to Quality Circle Time for beginners and those who want to improve their practice. Prepared to link with SEAL, this guide takes you through the key elements of the model, with a range of circle time plans and a mentor approach. Includes material adapted from 'The Circle Book' and 'Circle Time' by Jenny Mosley.

For information about training and courses please contact:
Jenny Mosley Consultancies
28A Gloucester Road
Trowbridge BA14 0AA
Tel: 01225 767157
Fax: 01225 755631
Email: circletime@jennymosley.co.uk

For a catalogue of other books published by Positive Press please contact:
Positive Press
28A Gloucester Road
Trowbridge BA14 0AA
Tel: 01225 719204
Fax: 01225 712187
Email: positivepress@jennymosley.co.uk
Website: www.circle-time.co.uk